IN THE WORLD BUT NOT OF IT

IN THE WORLD
BUT NOT OF IT

One Family's Militant Faith and the History of
Fundamentalism in America

Brett Grainger

Walker & Company
New York

Published by Walker Publishing Company, Inc., New York
Distributed to the trade by Macmillan

All papers used by Walker & Company are natural, recyclable products made
from wood grown in well-managed forests. The manufacturing processes conform to the environmental regulations of the country of origin.

LIBRARY OF CONGRESS CATALOGING-IN-PUBLICATION DATA HAS BEEN APPLIED FOR.

ISBN-10: 0-8027-1559-1
ISBN-13: 978-0-8027-1559-3

Visit Walker & Company's Web site at www.walkerbooks.com

First U.S. edition 2008

1   3   5   7   9   10   8   6   4   2

Typeset by Westchester Book Group
Printed in the United States of America by Quebecor World Fairfield

For my parents

The world has hated them because they are not of the world, just as I am not of the world. I do not pray that you should take them out of the world, but that you should keep them from the evil one.

—JOHN 17:14–15

I'm not living in this world, I'm dying in it.

—JOHN NELSON DARBY

CONTENTS

IN THE WORLD BUT NOT OF IT

Introduction

THE F-WORD

WHEN I TOLD my mother I would be writing a book about Christian fundamentalism, the first thing she said was "Oh, that's nice. What is a fundamentalist?"

I couldn't believe my ears. "Mom," I said, "our whole family are fundamentalists." My parents had grown up in the Plymouth Brethren, a small and militant band of believers who had, during the second half of the nineteenth century, helped to erect a number of the intellectual pillars of fundamentalism. During my childhood in the 1970s, I had consistently been taught to read the Bible as the literal word of God, inerrant in every detail, and to regard movies, pop music, and other forms of popular entertainment as "worldly"—a word that suggested a state of compromise and contamination. How could my mother not know what a fundamentalist was?

But the more I thought about it, the more her question made a certain kind of sense. I couldn't remember a time when anyone in the family had described himself as a fundamentalist. The Brethren forsook labels, preferring generic titles such as *Christian* or *believer*. Only in college did I begin to associate the religious culture of my childhood with something called fundamentalism. I learned to regard fundamentalists as stubborn relics of a pre-enlightened age. Against modern liberal values of freedom and equality, they sowed seeds of intolerance and superstition, a band of hardened zealots waging a rearguard action against Western progress.

Though my sympathies had drifted to liberalism, something about this characterization rang hollow. The Brethren I knew were not extremists, but everyday men and women who lived lives of quiet piety. Their religious beliefs were no more irrational than those professed by Christians for millennia. Their cultural attitudes were cloistered but not xenophobic; the work of evangelism constantly brought them into contact with other races and cultures. Believers were suspicious of higher education, and yet they placed an inordinate stress on literacy and daily study of the Scriptures. And though they were out of step with mainstream attitudes on issues such as abortion, they had no desire to infiltrate the government and impose their religious vision on the world. The Brethren were "separatists," which meant that they avoided all political activity, even voting, as impure. In day-to-day life, it would have been difficult to distinguish a believer from a nonbeliever. The Brethren were entirely at home in the middle-class world of shopping malls, supermarkets, and subdivisions. They dressed the same as non-believers, sent their children to the same schools, toiled in the same positions. But deep in their hearts, the Brethren saw themselves as outsiders, a holy remnant that stood apart from the world.

As the historian George Marsden has noted, fundamentalists are "preachers of paradox."[1] Believers are constantly harmonizing the contradictions of tradition and modernity. In one and the same breath, America might be celebrated as Zion or condemned as Babylon. Believers might be described as a "faithful remnant," a persecuted and purified elect, or a "moral majority" exercising influence over legislators on Capitol Hill. This willingness to embrace paradox has given fundamentalists an astonishing flexibility. With each new generation, believers rework the ancient clay to contemporary molds. Fundamentalists describe their faith as a steady rock in the swirling seas of modern life, but everything about their streamlined, no-nonsense Christianity—its practices, beliefs, and attitude to the world—is in a constant state of struggle and evolution.

For much of the twentieth century, the stubborn persistence of fundamentalism was explained by social factors. H. Richard Niebuhr once called fundamentalism a "religion of the dispossessed."[2] They were the losers of history: the masses of socially marginalized and culturally benighted souls who had been left behind in the long march of Western civilization. The most common version of this explanation, known as the secularization thesis, held that conservative religious beliefs would wither with the spread of modernity. Yet the numbers tell a different story. Between 1960 and 2000, the Southern Baptist Convention, one of the country's most influential fundamentalist denominations, grew from 10 million to 17 million members, while membership in the liberal Episcopalian Church fell from 3.5 million to 2 million. The phenomenal growth of Christian fundamentalism can't comfortably be explained as the product of mass cultural neurosis. For many millions of Americans, militant faith provides a persuasive answer to the question of what it is to be modern. People become fundamentalists for reasons, often quite good ones, and it behooves us to listen to some of those reasons before passing judgment.

My mother's question—"What is a fundamentalist?"—would have been more easily answered in the first half of the twentieth century. A fundamentalist was someone who affirmed the historic "five fundamentals of faith" as first set down during the Niagara Bible Conference movement of 1878–87 and formalized in 1910 by the General Assembly of the Presbyterian Church: the inerrancy of the Bible, the virgin birth of Jesus, the doctrine of substitutionary atonement (the idea that "Jesus died for our sins"), Jesus' bodily resurrection, and the doctrine of miracles (or alternatively, the imminent Second Coming of Jesus). The name was coined in 1920 by Curtis Lee Laws, the editor of a Baptist newspaper, who wrote that a fundamentalist was someone willing to do "battle royal" for the faith.[3] But the Scopes Monkey Trial of 1925, in which a biology teacher named John T. Scopes was convicted of teaching evolution in Dayton, Tennessee, turned fundamentalism into an F-word. The skeptical Northeastern journalists sent to cover the trial depicted the antievolution forces that congregated in Dayton as a superstitious rabble of slack-jawed yokels, creating a cultural cliché that would dog the movement into the early twenty-first century.

Already by the 1950s, the pejorative associations had reached such a degree that a young revivalist named Billy Graham disavowed the F-word in favor of *new evangelical*—a term that retained the doctrinal emphases of fundamentalism without its reputation for divisiveness and belligerence. Graham avoided politics and focused on saving souls, and succeeded in bringing

"Bible-believing Christians" back into respectable conversation. Groups such as Campus Crusade for Christ made inroads at colleges and universities, places that fundamentalists had alternately abandoned and been forced out of in the early decades of the twentieth century.

In the 1970s, the F-word made a comeback. Reacting to the perceived moral decline in America hastened by the antiwar movement and the sexual revolution, a new generation of flashy televangelists—preachers such as Jerry Falwell, Pat Robertson, and D. James Kennedy—blended the savvy of the neo-evangelicals with a renewed moral outrage. But their effort to reclaim the positive connotations of fundamentalism was hindered by political events on the far side of the world. In 1978, the Iranian religious leader Ayatollah Khomeini led a revolt against the Shah that resulted in the creation of an Islamic theocracy. In press reports, it became common to read of "Islamic fundamentalism." The terrorist attacks of September 11, 2001, helped to further broaden the definition of a fundamentalist to include virtually any agent of religious violence and intolerance.

Today, the majority of those who in previous decades would proudly have called themselves fundamentalists publicly shun the name. *Evangelical* has become the one-size-fits-all descriptor for Protestant Christians who, in general, ascribe to conservative moral values and a theology that centers on evangelism, the work of "winning souls." The result has been a loss of clarity. While all Christian fundamentalists are evangelicals, not all evangelicals are the same. Fundamentalists, for example, differ from mainstream evangelicals, who do their best to "get along" with American culture, taking a conciliatory tone and downplaying areas of discord. They put evangelism ahead of purity. Fundamentalists reverse that equation. As much or more of their energy is devoted to pursuing holiness and resisting worldly influences. They spend a greater amount of time worrying over the decline of "moral values," defending the Bible from attack, and speculating about the end of the world.

Despite sharing a number of concerns, Christian fundamentalists are not easy to define as a movement. For one thing, they are highly decentralized, with no center outside that of the Bible itself. While often described as homogeneous, fundamentalism is no monolith but a sprawling collection of competing values and contradictory instincts. Believers may share a core set of beliefs, but they are deeply divided over how and to what extent Christians should participate in mainstream society. For some, America has a special destiny as a chosen nation. For others, it has been singled out for destruction. Some believers serve in the military, while others are pacifists. Some condemn materialism, while others see conspicuous consumption as evidence of God's grace. Some feel called to enter politics, while others refuse even to cast a vote, lest they become entangled in worldly concerns. To make things messier, many believe various combinations of all of the above.

A good place to start is the definition offered by George Marsden, who described a fundamentalist as "an evangelical who is angry about something."[4] Marsden's insight is that fundamentalism has less to do with a set body of doctrine than a particular attitude or tone, a way of being in the world. What fundamentalists are angry about is secular modernity, a period that began roughly in the second half of the nineteenth century, when the mingled streams of industrialism, the Enlightenment, Romanticism, secularization, and the Second Scientific Revolution wrought unprecedented changes in virtually every area of American society. Many of the basic tenets of Christian orthodoxy—ancient notions of physical resurrection and the divinity of Jesus, among others—underwent dramatic redefinition as liberal ministers and denominations struggled to remain "relevant." Those who resisted these innovations took up an old banner, the call to purify the church of worldly influences, to be "in the world but not of it."

Many histories of Christian fundamentalism begin with the turbulent 1920s and the Scopes Monkey Trial, which put fundamentalists on the national stage. However, by 1925, the year of *Scopes v. State*, the basic template of Christian fundamentalism—millenarianism, biblical literalism, doctrinal purity, antievolutionism, Christian Zionism—had been kicking around for nearly half a century.[5] By paying particular attention to that neglected early history, I hope to show how fundamentalism was both an attempt to preserve earlier beliefs and practices *and* a radical break from what came before. Like the Counter-Reformation of the 1600s, which aimed to secure Catholic tradition against the innovations of Protestant theology and the liberalizing effects of the Renaissance, fundamentalism fell prey to the paradox of conservatism described by G. K. Chesterton. "All conservatism," Chesterton writes, "is based upon the idea that if you leave things alone you leave them as they are. But you do not . . . If you leave a white post alone it will soon be a black post. If you particularly want it to be white you must be always painting it again; that is, you must be always having a revolution."[6]

For more than a century, the defenders of old-time religion have engaged in a revolutionary reworking of the fundamentals of Christian faith. Their brand of orthodoxy is a simulacrum of modernity, a streamlined architecture, composed of rational lines, simplified forms, and a stark palette. Contrary to conventional wisdom, fundamentalists are not interested in returning to medieval times. They are among the most adept pupils of the modern age, copying and recasting its designs for their own purposes. What is remarkable about fundamentalists is not how they resist the intellectual habits of liberal society—rationalism, individualism, pluralism, alienation—but how well they exemplify the modern condition. The fact that fundamentalism offers believers an alternate way of being modern suggests that its future depends not merely on how believers respond to perennial concerns such as the reliability of Scripture but on how secular modernity defends itself against its own internal challenges, particularly those represented by postmodernity.

Chapter 1

WAITING FOR GOD

O N   S U N D A Y, September 11, 1988, my grandparents spent the day in their living room in a small town in northern Ontario, waiting for Jesus Christ to return and rapture them to heaven.

By then, I was sixteen and had already fallen away from the Plymouth Brethren, the small fundamentalist sect in which my grandfather was a lay preacher, what believers called a laboring brother. Years later, I wondered what might have led an otherwise sensible man to chance everything, his reputation and livelihood, on such a hope. Playing out the events in my mind, I wondered how he and my grandmother had passed the day.

During the Rapture, the first thing my grandfather would have expected was the trump of the archangel. A brassy, triumphant staccato, perhaps, of the sort that accompanied a charge of the light cavalry. But maybe the call would sound less familiar, uncanny, a subsonic vibration transmitted on a bandwidth only the faithful had been tuned to receive. This was, after all, the "Secret Rapture." Next came the fun part—the flying. We had been told that the dead in Christ would rise first, followed by the living. The Rapture filled my mind with questions. Did you leave your clothes behind? If so, were you naked? If you had a spiritual body, would you still feel the wind in your hair? Did you float up like a balloon or explode across the sky like a human cannonball? And would the sky be clear and blue or dark and overcast, like the pillar of cloud in Exodus that followed the Israelites during their march through the wilderness?

My grandfather was not a man to trouble himself with such questions. He had risen early that Sunday morning, shaved, put on his good suit—a gray two-piece, bought off-the-rack and on sale—and knotted one of the many garish paisley ties that his wife had made for him. My grandmother put on a long skirt and a wide-brimmed hat. They ate breakfast together, then spent a time in prayer in the living room of the brick bungalow. The Brethren elders had asked my grandfather not to come to church that morning. His predictions had caused too much tension among the believers.

My grandfather read his Bible, lingering over the prophecies of Daniel and Revelation, and the cryptic warnings that run like an erratic red stitch through the Gospels and the letters of Paul: "For the Lord himself shall descend from heaven with a shout, with the voice of the archangel, and with the trump of God: and the dead in Christ shall rise first; Then we which are alive shall be caught up together with them in the clouds, to meet the Lord in the air. Wherefore comfort one another with these words."

He read to comfort himself. Then he prayed. He prayed for his six children and for their families, for the grandchildren who were still dead in their sins, that the Spirit would strive with them, roiling the waters of the heart until they acknowledged their utter depravity and professed their faith in the cross of Jesus

Christ, in the blood shed at Calvary. He prayed for the Lord's glorious appearing, for the Rapture of the saints, for the promise of a new heaven and a new earth.

My grandmother played a hymn at the organ, then, feeling restless, took up her knitting. An old clock ticked away the countdown. She paused in midstitch, displeased to realize that she would be leaving a work half finished. Setting aside her needles, she resolved to make some last-minute phone calls to loved ones.

One of the calls was to my mother. My grandmother told her that we should help ourselves to her homemade preserves and ginger cookies. "We won't be needing them," she said gaily.

This upset my mother. As she later pointed out, it insinuated that our family would be stuck with last summer's chutney while the saints feasted in glory. "Can you imagine the nerve?" she asked my father. A happy-go-lucky cowboy in greasy blue coveralls with a handlebar mustache, he raised his eyebrows and shrugged his shoulders, as if to say, "What are you going to do?" then returned to his basement workshop to bottle a batch of dandelion wine.

Such bad habits had brewed uncertainty in the mind of his parents. Since adolescence, my father had waged a cautious rebellion against the Brethren, needling them with his worldly behavior—growing long sideburns, smoking cigarettes, getting a motorbike—but always showing up on time for gospel meeting. My mother found his ungodliness impossible to resist. She had pursued the path of least resistance among the Brethren, submitting to the Protestant rituals of conversion and baptism under the eye of her pious and overbearing father. When she married the prodigal son of a prominent preacher, my mother launched a quiet rebellion. She never liked my father's homemade wine, but she was glad that he did.

The day wore on. My grandfather sat in an ancient recliner in the corner of the living room. The chair elevated his bad leg, which he'd injured in a childhood accident while playing with a loaded rifle. With his long legs suspended in midair, he appeared to have already taken leave of the earth. But as hours passed and the skies stubbornly refused to part, his body seemed to acquire more mass. His gray eyebrows weighed on his brow bushy and unkempt like a bird's nest, his mind all wheels, turning.

In such moments, a man can take stock of his life. He may have looked back on his sacrifices, everything he had done to separate himself from a sinful world and preach the gospel of repentance. Like many Brethren, during the Second World War he had rejected military service and spent years in a government logging camp. After the war, he embarked on a second exile in northern Quebec, taking along his young wife and newborn daughter. The winters were so cold it froze the milk in the baby's bottle. During the day, he studied French so that when evening came, he could go out into the streets and carry the gospel to the benighted Catholics.

It was his trial in the wilderness, a time of testing that prepared him for a life of itinerant ministry, a half century of living hand to mouth, earning what his tongue could wring from a handful of tightfisted believers and sending it home to a wife and six kids he barely knew. He waged a nightly battle for men's souls, preaching himself hoarse in mosquito-filled canvas tents, clapboard community halls, a stranger's living room, anywhere two or three gathered together in the Lord's name.

He might have spent a good while in this sort of soul-searching. Slowly he became aware of the shadows falling across the living room carpet. His wife hobbled into the kitchen on her plastic hip and stopped in front of the sink, where a roast was thawing. She'd taken it from the freezer that morning. Just in case. She looked out the kitchen window upon the world they had both been so eager to shrug off: the garden of carrots and turnips and corn, the pallid tangle of birches, the rolling trapezoid of lawn. She clipped beans at the counter, while her husband rose and looked out toward the river in the gathering dark, its cold, silent course lost to human understanding.

According to one poll, 20 percent of Americans are waiting for the Rapture. One way to account for this extraordinarily high figure is to point to the totems of twenty-first-century cultural anxiety—fears of Islamic terrorism, economic turmoil, the perceived breakdown of traditional moral values. Conventional wisdom holds that millennial expectation spikes during periods of great social upheaval.

The Bible has always provided Christians with a lightning rod to channel their angst. In times of trouble, its ancient prophecies, as variable as a Rorschach inkblot, are laid open upon the table and studied. While suffering persecution and martyrdom under the Romans, the earliest Christians anticipated the return of Jesus within their immediate generation. After a few centuries, however, believers had largely accommodated themselves to Roman culture and no longer expected that the savior's return would be imminent or even strictly necessary.

The decisive turn came during the fourth century, when Constantine baptized his Roman Empire Christian. Rather than project the millennial kingdom into the future, many came to regard it as a present reality. Augustine of Hippo framed the prophecies of Revelation as an allegory for the Church's victory over paganism. Belief in a literal Second Coming dwindled to a minority position that enjoyed periodic revivals over the proceeding millennium, whenever plagues, natural disasters, or significant calendrical moments called into question the future of civilization.

During the Reformation, literalism made a comeback. The catastrophic warfare, charges of rank apostasy among the clergy, and widespread political instability seemed to fit the Bible's description of the last days. In Germany and England, the visions contained in the book of Daniel inspired reformers to lead political revolts against the established powers. During the 1520s, a former student of Martin Luther's named Thomas Müntzer called himself a new Daniel and led a peasant uprising in Germany, through which he hoped to establish the kingdom of God. In England, the political chaos that followed the execution of Charles I in 1649 sparked a decade of millennial fever. Almost daily, new religious groups were formed with colorful names such as the Diggers, the Ranters, the Levellers, and the Fifth Monarchy Men. The last group took its name from the book of Daniel, in which the prophet interprets a dream by King Nebuchadnezzar. In the dream, the king sees a massive statue made of five different metals, which the Fifth Monarchy Men interpreted to represent five earthly empires, four of which—the Assyrian, Persian, Greek, and Roman—had already passed. The fifth and final empire, the reign of "King Jesus," as they called him, would begin in 1666. When the Fifth Monarchy Men tried to seize control of London, Oliver Cromwell had the leadership rounded up and executed.

Another outbreak of millennial fever followed the French Revolution of 1789. As revolutionaries waged a root-and-branch war on Christianity—beheading priests and restarting the calendar at Year Zero—British and American Protestants debated the signs of the times and set probable dates for Christ's imminent return. In America, the most popular prophet of the early nineteenth century was a self-educated farmer from upper New York State named William Miller. After applying numerology to the scriptures, Miller concluded that Jesus was coming back in 1843. A great many Millerites sold their homes and farms to become itinerant preachers and in a short time enlisted as many as one hundred thousand followers. When Miller's first date passed uneventfully, the prophet apologized and revised his prediction, explaining that he hadn't taken the Jewish calendar into account. The new date was set for Yom Kippur of the following year—a day that became known as the Great Disappointment. Most of the Millerites wandered away and returned to their former lives; those who remained loyal came up with ways to rationalize the failed prophecy and went on to found the Seventh-Day Adventist Church. In his memoirs, Miller confided that if he had to do it all over again, he would. "I confess my error," he wrote, "and acknowledge my disappointment."[1]

After the Millerite scandal, American Christians became warier of the dangers of End Times fever and especially of date fixers. As the end of the century approached, Americans faced cultural and social changes of an unprecedented magnitude: waves of Jewish and Catholic immigrants, rapid industrialization, and new challenges to biblical authority and traditional doctrines such as the resurrection. For many conservative believers, Christianity and the modern age were traveling in opposite directions. In a bid to defend orthodoxy, they turned to a recent doctrinal innovation: the Rapture. The basic idea had been worked out in the 1830s by an itinerant Brethren preacher from England named John Nelson Darby. Unlike Miller, who saw prophecy coming true in daily events, Darby argued that none of the Bible's promises would come to pass before the Rapture. Though Jesus could return at any moment, there was no magic date hidden in the scriptures—in other words, no way to disprove the Rapture. Darby had found a way to walk the tightrope of millennial hope without tipping over into disappointment.

"Wait until I come again," Jesus said to his disciples, and the Brethren complied by treating his words as the eleventh commandment. To wait was the fulfillment of the law. *Expecto ergo sum*: I wait, therefore I am. All time was pregnant with expectation. For two and a half hours every Sunday morning, the Brethren waited in silence for the Holy Spirit to move a brother to stand and pray or lead a hymn. Believers hedged their vacation plans with the caveat "If the Lord be not come." Parents instructed children to subordinate any love or ambition to the Great Hope, the promise of sudden spiritual abduction.

From my earliest days growing up across the river from my grandparents, I was raised to wait upon the Rapture of the saints. Apocalypse was a distant cloud always on the horizon. In the blinking of an eye, everyone I loved could be torn from me, leaving streets suddenly full of driverless cars and uneven road-hockey teams. On Sunday nights, my grandfather would crane his long frame out over the plywood pulpit and fix me with his burning eyes, his voice breaking as he described the horrors awaiting those who tarried in sin. Even tonight, he cried, the Lord might return to claim his own. Was I ready?

Like many preachers, he used visual aids to illustrate his sermons. I remember a colorful chart called "The Two Roads and the Two Destinies." It had been hand-painted on a long canvas sheet, which he unfurled and tacked up on the wall behind the pulpit. The map had a wild tangle of arrows and paths leading to future events. To a child it looked like a complicated version of Chutes and Ladders. Everyone started on the Broad Road, a wide path that sloped down toward a looming black obelisk marked Death. Once past it, sinners continued a downhill slide past the Judgment of the Great White Throne and came to rest in the Lake of Fire, a bright red spot in the map's bottom right-hand corner.

A person's only hope was to pass through a bright yellow door, located halfway down the Broad Road. The door, representing salvation, opened on a narrow path that skirted the top of the obelisk and climbed straight to Heaven. Heaven was full of all manner of strange events—the Judgment Seat of Christ, the Marriage Supper of the Lamb—while just below, the unsaved who remained on Earth endured the seven-year Tribulation, the wars of Gog and Magog, the destruction of Babylon, and the Battle of Armageddon.

My grandfather's map fixed itself in my heart. I lay in bed for hours, plotting my progress down the Broad Road, wondering how many turns I had left to play. One day when I was ten, I came home from school and found the house empty. I knew my parents would be at work, but somehow I convinced myself they had been raptured. Seized with terror, I phoned my grandparents.

So long as I could reach at least one of them, I knew that there was still time.

My grandmother answered. Hearing her singsong warble drained the fear from my body. I was suddenly embarrassed, and hung up without saying a word.

The Brethren had no priesthood or professional clergy, no seminaries, no official theology, no creed outside Scripture. Practically speaking, this meant any "brother" (a baptized male believer) could get up in Gospel Meeting and say whatever came into his head. My cousin Dick, who drove a bulldozer and had a pet raccoon—he kept him in a doghouse on a long chain—had as much right to expound on the complicated visions of Daniel and Revelation as my grandfather, who had been studying prophecy most of his adult life.

Even Dick understood that there were rules when interpreting Scripture, however unspoken they might be. Prophetic Rule Number One: under no condition might a believer attempt to fix the Second Coming to a definite date. As Jesus said, we can read the signs of the times, but no one knows the day or the hour of his return.

So in 1988, when my grandfather announced that Jesus was coming back in September during Rosh Hashanah, we were stunned. My parents tried not to talk about it in front of me, but I sensed their embarrassment. It was clear my grandfather was sincere—it wasn't clear what he would gain if he was right, but if he was wrong, he stood to lose everything he had worked for. What made him go against tradition?

I lay much of the blame on my father's brother. Uncle Jack was a salesman for a drug company with a pair of tunneling blue eyes and a smile like a chrome bumper. One day, Jack came across a pamphlet called *88 Reasons Why the Rapture Could Be in 1988* by Edgar Whisenant. Like most popular prophecy writers, Whisenant had no formal training in the Bible. He was an engineer who had at one time worked for NASA. Whisenant took the no-nonsense approach to problem solving he'd learned in engineering school and applied it to Scripture. Numbers were mined from passages all over the Bible and ruthlessly processed until they produced a result, a simple formula that could predict the date of the Rapture as reliably as the next lunar eclipse.

Uncle Jack was so persuaded by Whisenant's simple logic that he went door-to-door in an effort to convince his neighbors to settle their affairs with God. My grandfather came on board and used his influence to spread the message from the pulpit. He bought himself a new car, a luxury he could hardly afford on his meager salary. "Why worry?" he reasoned. They would never have to pay for it. Such flippancy soon divided the family. I remember a fight between my grandfather and one of my aunts, who had just bought new clothes and school supplies for her children. "Why are you buying them stuff for school?" he asked. "They won't be here!"

He had as much trouble converting the rest of the Brethren. In the assemblies on his regular circuit, his preaching was met by stern glares and stony silence. In one town, the elders rebuked him for presuming upon the inscrutable will of God. Uncle Jack also met with resistance from fellow Brethren in his assembly. Angry, drawn-out debates resulted in a slow exodus of families ground down by the grandstanding. A few months before the appointed day, the elders reached the end of their patience. They gave Jack an ultimatum: be silent or face excommunication.

Jack was confident and used to getting his way, so he fixed his high beams on one of the elders, a middle-aged mechanic. The elder lacked Jack's charm and knowledge of Scripture, and Jack did his best to browbeat him, describing elaborate private visions that he said confirmed his predictions. But the elder would not be moved.

"Look at all the confusion this has caused, Jack," the elder said. "God is not the author of confusion. For that reason, I have to say that you're wrong."

In the end, Jack had no choice but to submit to the will of the assembly. The day of atonement came and went, and the following Sunday, Jack got up in front of everyone and gave a half-hearted apology. Afterward, the millennial fires burned down to embers. Folks went back to living each moment as if Jesus might come, without really expecting that he would. A number of the elders resigned, complaining of exhaustion. The mechanic seemed particularly affected. Believers noted how he seemed nervous and emotionally distant, how he refused phone calls and visitors. Some passed the rumor that he had been seen coming out of a local tavern. Others spoke of depression. Not long afterward, he broke from the Brethren.

Throughout my childhood, my father was alternately dismissive and hostile toward religion, feelings that were closely tied to his relationship with my grandfather. Many full-time preachers rarely saw their children. They stayed in touch through letters like the following one, written when my father was seven:

Dear Daddy,

Thank you for the picture of the black bear. I have had bron-
chitis and I am not doing as I'm told. I hope you are having a
nice time. I have not been reading my bible very much. I have
been praying. I am glad to hear that some girls are interested in
getting saved. Bye for now.

Love, Malcolm

In 1958, when my father was eight, he wrote again.

Dear Daddy,

I am glad many are getting saved and Mummy is too. I will be
glad when you are at home. Hope you are having a nice time
and I want to know when you are coming home. ~~I am going
to start and behave before you come home~~.

With love, your Son, Malcolm

A note from my grandmother runs across the top of the letter:
"Malcolm crumpled this up after I crossed out the end." In the
margin next to the offending line, she wrote, "He does not mean
to keep his word."

My grandmother kept a running tally of the children's misbe-
haviors during my grandfather's absences. When he came home,
the first matter of business was to get out the strap. Malcolm
would laugh during his beating, his insolence winning him more
of his father's undivided attention.

When my father was fifteen, the ritual was reversed. After

another long trip, my grandfather came home and reached for his belt. This time, Malcolm struck back, wrestling and then pinning him to the ground. He told his father that he wouldn't let him back up until he promised never to hit him again. Startled and overpowered, my grandfather gave his word.

At home, my father contained his emotions like a dam holding back a great river. Anger and joy were muted colors. In family pictures, he always smiled but never showed his teeth. He was prone to black moods, especially before a stretch of night shifts at the factory. I learned to tread softly. On his days off, he retreated to the sanctum of the garage or to his workshop in the basement, making him an ever-present absence in the house. I wondered what would happen when the river finally broke loose.

When I was seventeen, my father was touched by a spiritual awakening. Why he chose this particular moment to get religion is a bit of a mystery. Perhaps it was a classic midlife crisis—at the time, he was a year or two short of forty. It may also have been a defensive reaction to my grandfather's humiliation in 1988. Barely a year had passed since the scandal, and as Dad admitted, it was hard to watch his father be ostracized by the same believers who had once idolized and feared him. There were other triggers. For years, my dad had watched his brothers take more prominent roles in the assembly, preaching and leading the prayer meeting, while he remained at the back of the hall with his arms crossed, a toothpick in his mouth. Almost without noticing, the youthful rebel had become a middle-aged family man whose problem with authority made it difficult to hold down a job. Rather than continue to kick against the pricks, he joined them.

Almost overnight, the scoffer became a spiritual seeker. He began regular disciplines of prayer and reading the Bible. He talked about his desire to be restored. The first step was to get baptized. When my father shared the news, I could barely believe it. My mother didn't say much, but I could tell she was even more surprised. He had always been her black sheep. Where was her forbidden fruit?

My grandparents rejoiced at the return of their prodigal son, though even in them, I sensed a measure of disbelief. It just didn't seem like Dad. Feelings bubbled out of him like a washing machine overloaded with detergent. He talked earnestly of his plans to preach the gospel, even of sharing a pulpit with his father. By this point, my grandfather had been welcomed back to many of the assemblies that had shunned him after the disastrous fallout of 1988. He'd even begun to tackle prophecy again, though his message focused on general signs of the times, mostly related to events in the Middle East. Saddam Hussein was stocking his arsenal and calling himself a new Nebuchadnezzar, the Babylonian king described in the book of Daniel, who conquered Jerusalem and destroyed the Temple. When Hussein announced his intention to rebuild Babylon, Nebuchadnezzar's ancient capital, my grandfather twitched with anticipation.

Meanwhile, my father set about making up for a misspent youth. His attendance at the Gospel Hall became scrupulous. He began to experiment with fasting. At home, he dispensed spiritual platitudes and confessed his failure to be a spiritual role model. I was pleased with the attention I was getting but uncomfortable with his new emotional liberty. One time, he came into my bedroom and asked forgiveness—for what, he didn't say. Then he began to cry. I was bewildered and muttered something about there being nothing to forgive, but my words didn't seem to reach him.

My mother heard the commotion. Taking him by the arm, like a little boy who'd lost his way, she led him out of the room. A water main had burst inside him. Feelings placed under pressure for so many years had found a way out.

Everything became more and more extreme. His experiment with fasting became a refusal to eat. His body withered and his shoulders slumped forward. The night shift messed with his internal clock, producing insomnia. Night and day became a constant waking blur. He began to hallucinate. While the rest of the family was having dinner, he would walk into the kitchen wild-eyed and unshaven, talking about his visions. He saw dead people he knew coming and going from heaven, twinkling in the sky like stars.

Late one night, I wandered out on the lawn to get some air and saw him in his pajamas, staring up at the sky. His eyes were unfocused, his face gaunt and sallow. He turned and acknowledged my presence, then raised a finger into the moonless night.

"You see those two stars?" he said, gesturing toward a constellation. "That star is my father. The one next to it is me."

"Okay," I said, as if I had a clue what he was talking about. Then I fled inside, leaving him alone in the dark.

As the oldest child, I carried a growing sense of dread, one born of responsibility. My father's behavior hadn't yet caused the family anything more than concern and occasional embarrassment. What would I do if there came a time when he presented an actual threat? Even in his weakened state, I doubted I was strong enough to pin him to the ground as he had his own father twenty-five years before. While Dad paced the floors, I wrestled with my fears, waiting for some kind of sign.

It came a few days later. I was in the kitchen with my mother when he came in the room. He seemed to have aged twenty years in a few months' time. In a ragged voice, he said he regretted that he had ever had children. I nodded slowly, then excused myself and went to the basement. With terrible clarity, I opened my father's workbench and pocketed a handful of shells, then climbed a stepladder into the rafters and brought down the rifle. I took the gun to my room, leaning it up against the wall just behind the door. Then, for the first time in years, I prayed.

When my grandfather preached about eternity, I often played a game with myself, an experiment in infinite regression. "If eternity lasts forever," I thought, "that means it's still going on . . . now." I held my breath and tried to imagine how eternity felt. It was like staring down a dark elevator shaft, or casting a line into a fast-flowing river. No matter how much line you started with, the hungry current would eat up the slack until your spool was empty and the reel locked up. Each time I played my little game, it left me charged with excitement and terror, the feeling of running flat out and hitting a glass wall.

As I got older, my early anxiety about the Rapture receded and was replaced by the secular angst of adolescence. St. John of the Apocalypse made way for the modern prophets of existentialism, Samuel Beckett and Albert Camus. When I read Beckett's *Waiting for Godot*, I was struck by the similarity in vocabulary and concerns: the universality of dread, the ambivalence of free will and mortality. This was the first time that many of the students in my public high school had wrestled with such basic human questions. For me, terror and dread already felt like old friends. When Beckett's two beggars, Vladimir and Estragon, argued whether

Godot was coming today, I thought of my grandparents in their living room, waiting for the sky to open.

In the summer of 1990, *U.S. News & World Report* announced that Saddam Hussein was "The World's Most Dangerous Man." My grandfather agreed, though he suspected Hussein was really only a puppet whose movements were guided by an invisible hand. A few months later, Iraqi armored columns rolled across the oil fields of Kuwait. Meeting minimal resistance, they subdued the country and began massing along the border of Saudi Arabia. Hussein compared himself to Saladin, the great Islamic warrior who conquered Jerusalem in the twelfth century, and promised to bury Israel under a cloud of chemical weapons. The UN condemned the occupation of Kuwait, and President George H. W. Bush dispatched three hundred thousand troops to the desert to draw a line in the sand. On the home front, a domestic crisis was brewing. My father could no longer work. Doctors placed him on long-term disability, and he spent his days in and out of bed. I sat in my room and looked at the rifle still resting in the corner.

That Christmas, nature seemed out of joint. Instead of snow squalls and ice-skating, the hayfields were blanketed in mud and the lakes refused to freeze. The newspapers were filled with wars and rumors of wars. The UN had given Iraq a deadline to withdraw from Kuwait, after which the United States and its allies were authorized to use all necessary force to dislodge the occupation. My grandfather, who had briefly become a presence in the house, went out on the road, preaching the coming kingdom. Dad's condition continued to deteriorate until the doctors finally decided to bring him to the hospital. He wasn't getting enough food; they wanted to be able to monitor him closely. My mother put on a brave face and said she thought everything would sort itself out once he got proper treatment. He was diagnosed as manic-depressive, which accounted for the dramatic highs and lows, the ecstatic pronouncements and tearful self-recriminations. He started taking lithium, though he complained of the side effects, the nausea, stomach cramps, and general disorientation.

One day in January, I came home from school and heard my mother talking on the phone. It was the hospital. Dad was missing. He'd left without telling anyone. The doctor was concerned he had stopped taking his medication. Desperately composed, my mother called her parents. Her voice was lost somewhere in her chest.

"Malcolm's vanished," she said. "I didn't know who to call."

Her father came and picked her up, and together they went looking for Dad. They found him walking down the side of the road, halfway home, lost in a hallucination. He was put in an ambulance and taken to the closest psychiatric hospital, which was two hours away.

That night, I ate dinner at home with my mother and brother. To relieve the silence, my brother turned on the radio. The reporter was describing a world bathed in fire. American heavy bombers were dropping their first payloads on Baghdad; guided missiles rained down like falling stars. The night sky burned phosphorescent. In Israel, a Scud landed in the atrium of a shopping mall. Across the desert, oil wells were uncapped and set ablaze, growing a forest of thin trunks that leafed in black canopies and blotted out the morning.

We spent the night in the living room listening to the world fall apart. A few years before, in his brick bungalow across the river, my grandfather had prayed for such an apocalypse. Though he had observed the letter of the eleventh commandment, "Wait until I come again," he had missed the spirit. For the Brethren, waiting was never a science but a spiritual condition, the antechamber to an appointment without fixed time or place. As most believers understood, the key to staving off disappointment was to live each day as if the world might end tomorrow, without every really thinking that it would.

In my case, the wait was over. The end had come, and life went on. In a way, I felt liberated, as if I had been released from a purgatory. I turned to my homework, which was to memorize a scene from *Waiting for Godot*. Vladimir was arguing with Estragon.

"We are not saints," says Vladimir, "but we have kept our appointment. How many people can boast as much?"

Chapter 2

THE WORD WAS GOD

THE VAST MAJORITY of the Brethren I knew had quiet lives. They sold shoes, answered phones, pumped gas, pushed pencils, poured concrete. They were the salt of the earth, mothers and fathers who put food on the table by the sweat of their brow. The physical trades garnered more respect than white-collar work. Carpentry was honored above medicine and law, as Jesus himself had been a carpenter. Wealth and status were ambiguous. Material prosperity could be a sign of God's blessing or a snare that hobbled a person's faith. One ambitious brother launched his own development company. When he became the largest real-estate developer in town, the Brethren praised his initiative. He bought a new Cadillac, built a mansion on the lake, and showered his wife in jewelry and furs. The more his business grew, the less time he had to attend the weekly meetings of the assembly. Believers began to murmur that mammon had been his undoing.

However lowly they might be in the eyes of the world, the Brethren had one critical advantage: the King James Bible. When believers gathered to share the Word, they left behind the tedium and disappointment of daily life and became heirs of a great cultural legacy. Their imagination was immersed in Scripture. The hero epics of Genesis, the wisdom of Proverbs and Ecclesiastes, the promises of Revelation, the psychology of the Psalms—by turns, hopeful and embittered, imprecatory and magnanimous— lent their hardscrabble lives a beauty and grace they might otherwise have lacked. The Bible compensated for their unpolished manners. It was more important to them than their cheap suits and unfashionable dresses.

When believers spoke with one another, the King James was their lingua franca. They used words long vanished from common speech: *yea* and *nay* and *verily* and *whosoever, thee* and *thou* and *thine*. They called one another brother and sister, as Paul had done in his epistles. Outside in the world, such antiquated habits would have sounded silly or affected. But on Sunday morning, when the plumber with a harelip stood and prayed over the bread and wine in seventeenth-century English, it seemed as though he had found his mother tongue.

The Brethren had little use for high culture. Few could recite any Shakespeare. Less than one in a hundred could tell Degas from Dalí. But every believer knew Matthew from Mark. They quoted memorable lines from the tragedy of King Saul or the Joseph cycle. It didn't matter that they were not wealthy or beautiful or cultivated. They possessed the greatest masterpiece in the English language.

What was it about the King James that inspired devotion? It wasn't simply the magnificence of its poetry. This was taken for granted. More important was its antiquity. Believers suspected that modern translations, though touted by those in the world as more accurate, were guilty of novelty and innovation. They heeded the warning contained in Revelation: "If any man shall take away from the words of the book of this prophecy, God shall take away his part out of the book of life, and out of the holy city, and from the things which are written in this book." Any believer could interpret the living Word, not just those schooled in theology and dead languages. Common sense was their Rosetta stone. This democratic sensibility could produce absurd results. I often heard the story of a young believer who tried to impress an elder by showing off his knowledge of Greek. The elder chastened him, "If the King James was good enough for Paul, then it's good enough for me."

Believers were defined by their cult of devotion to the Bible, their eagerness to defend and protect the Word. They compared themselves to the Protestant reformers who died at the stake for the right to read Holy Writ in the vernacular. In seventeenth-century New England, it was common for a family to own two or three copies of the Word, including one in a format large enough to be labeled "great." The Puritans burned statues of saints, then filled up their Bibles with images; some folio editions contained a woodcut of Adam and Eve, the first man looking jaunty in an Elizabethan beard and mustache.

Though separated by centuries, the Puritans were close cousins of the Brethren in their belief that the Bible was a book that was not a book, a totem of paper and animal hide that participated in a higher, transcendent reality. Paul told the Corinthians that his letters were written "not with ink, but with the Spirit of the living God," "not in tables of stone, but in fleshly tables of the heart." The evidence was in the transforming effect that the Bible had upon the believer. The Word entered through the ear or the eye and penetrated the heart. Reading became a sacrament. When believers opened the Bible, they entered sacred space.

Everything in the daily life of the Brethren revolved around reading and digesting the Word. They lived off the Bible the way the Great Plains Indians lived off the buffalo. No part was waste. Horns, spleen, tail—everything had its proper use and purpose. All Scripture was inspired of God and worthy for instruction. Even the vast intestinal stretches of I Chronicles, the endless coils of *begats*, were laid in the sun to dry, then used to carry water. Not a day passed when they did not search the Scriptures for comfort or correction. The Word waited on the nightstand. It stared down from bookcases and dozed in glove compartments. Women carried a small, tidy volume in their purses. The men's were considerably larger. A believer's Bible was expected to age at roughly the same pace as his body. Elderly brothers carried copies that were battered and falling to pieces, with sagging spines and missing pages. Such Bibles were highly prized. They marked a man well acquainted with the Word. My grandfather's Bible was little more than a patch of rawhide wrapped around a ragged sheaf of pages. The binding was broken and whole chapters were missing or out of order, but he always seemed to be able to find what he needed.

A man's Bible was more than a general revelation to humanity. It was the tally of a soul's particular walk with God, the transcript of an open-ended inquiry into truth. Though the canon was closed, believers were constantly adding to their Bibles, filling the margins with private commentaries like the rabbis who composed the Talmud. My grandfather's copy had so many notes, underlinings, and cross-references that at times it was hard to make out the biblical text.

Behind the pulpit, a Bible was a preacher's primary performance aid. They were rubbed, pummeled, coddled, slapped, stroked, pressed to lips and foreheads, squeezed tightly against the chest. It wasn't enough for a believer to love his Bible; he had to maul it, commune with it, coax and woo it, beat it with open palms as though pounding on the doors of heaven to open and divulge their secrets. A brother could be so bold because he trusted in his heart that every believer who read the Bible could know the mind of God.

They were people of the book. It wasn't good works that acquainted a soul with divinity, but reading and meditating upon Scripture. But the same faith that nurtured literacy was also suspicious of education. Believers had to be careful to regulate the sort of things they read. It was dangerous to have strange books around. Without knowing it, you might prostrate your mind before something unholy. When I told my grandfather that I had discovered literature, he was gravely concerned. "Why would you waste your time reading something that isn't true?" he asked.

To know the mind of God, a believer had to spend time with the Word every day. Each night after dinner, my grandparents read the chapter from Proverbs that corresponded with the day of the month. Afterward, they would linger at the table, weighing each word in their hearts. As you read, you tried to give each word the same weight, no matter how strange or opaque it might seem. You read with reverence and humility, like a Levite approaching the temple to make sacrifice. Behind the black curtain of type lay the Holy of Holies, the innermost chamber where God's presence dwelt.

I knew believers who would stay with a difficult verse for hours, wrestling with it like Jacob wrestled the angel until it bestowed a blessing. Believers read from Genesis to Revelation. They read until they knew Scripture better than they knew their neighbor or spouse, better than a chemist knows the periodic table. As a child in Sunday school, I carried a small folded card marked with empty squares. Each week, I received a new sticker containing a Bible verse to memorize over the coming week. By the next Sunday, if I knew it by heart, the teacher would stamp my card with a gold star and give me a new verse to memorize. Such drills were like weight training. You started at the lowest level—"Jesus wept," "Search the Scriptures"—and slowly increased your load until you could bench-press entire chapters. After years of training, the memory became toned and responsive. A believer could fieldstrip a Bible and put it back together blindfolded with one arm tied behind his back. When that day came, you woke up and realized you didn't need the book; the Word lived inside you.

No institution has done more to influence how American fundamentalists read the Bible than Dallas Theological Seminary. Since 1924, Dallas has produced many of the country's leading preachers and Bible teachers—such people as J. Dwight Pentecost, John Walvoord, Charles Swindoll, Tony Evans, Charles Ryrie, and Hal Lindsey. Dallas is the West Point of fundamentalism, training up spiritual warriors to battle the powers and principalities of the modern age with the sword of Scripture. Each year, the faculty sign a twelve-page doctrinal statement that begins with an article on the authority of the Bible: "We believe that 'all Scripture is given by inspiration of God' . . . in the sense that holy men of God 'were moved by the Holy Spirit to write the very words of Scripture . . . We believe that the whole Bible in the originals is therefore without error." Everyone at Dallas Theological Seminary is a biblical literalist.

A Gallup poll from 2007 showed that about one third of Americans believe the Bible is the actual word of God and is to be taken literally word for word—a level only slightly lower than several decades ago.[1] Yet, strange as it seems, literalists don't always take the Bible literally. When Jesus says, "I am the door," no believer would interpret the verse to mean that the savior is a piece of wood set on hinges. When literalists read the Psalms, they read it as poetry, allowing for rhetorical devices such as allegory and metaphor. But when they come to the Gospel accounts of Jesus' miracles or the story of Moses parting the Red Sea in Exodus, literalists take what they find at face value. In 1958, Dwight Pentecost, a professor of theology at Dallas, summarized literalism this way: "When the plain sense of Scripture makes common sense, seek no other sense."[2]

Fundamentalists hold sacred the notion that individual believers have the right and duty to interpret the Scriptures for themselves. This democratic sensibility, which is as old as the Reformation, is one of the reasons for literalism's appeal and the source of its heavy anti-intellectual streak. As one twentieth-century fundamentalist put it, "The Scriptures are not for the erudite, but for the simple-minded . . . All the material[s] needed for our understanding of the matter are contained in the Bible itself."[3]

"Every man becomes his own interpreter," says John Hannah, a professor of church history at Dallas. "We can open the Bible and find its deepest treasures without education. There is a sense in which that is true. But there is a sense in which that is disastrous."

One warm Texas morning in October, Hannah's colleague

J. Scott Horrell was teaching the doctrine of divine inspiration to the roughly 150 students enrolled in Introduction to Christian Theology. Most of the seminarians were dressed in what the student handbook calls "professional casual attire," though a handful wore T-shirts and jeans. Each had a Bible. Horrell is slight of body, with a gray mustache and a band of dark hair that runs around the back of his head. When lecturing, he favors folksy stories and illustrations, like a pastor giving a sermon. After Horrell opened in prayer, he began to extemporize, saying he sympathized with those who have trouble today accepting that the Bible is divinely inspired. For example, he said, each of the gospel writers offers a different chronology of the life of Jesus. How could the Bible contradict itself and still be the inerrant word of God?

The class read aloud a definition of biblical inspiration by Charles Ryrie, a famous graduate of the seminary: "God superintended human authors so that, using their own personalities, they composed and recorded without error his message in the words of the original manuscripts."[4] What this meant, Horrell said, was that divine inspiration doesn't erase the individuality of the scribe; God allowed the Gospel writers to tell Jesus' story in their own way, shaping the details according to the particular themes that each considered the most important. Their differences did not limit their ability to present objective truth; rather, their subjectivity was the chosen vehicle for the eternal.

Horrell asked volunteers to read a long list of Bible verses that supported biblical inspiration. The first was the most common of fundamentalist "proof texts," 2 Timothy 3:16: "Every scripture inspired of God is also profitable for teaching, for reproof, for correction, for instruction which is in righteousness." Horrell said the verse would give them tools to explain what inspiration did *not* mean. "Inspiration in the Bible does not mean that man wrote those manuscripts and then God came in later and inspired it," Horrell said. "It does not mean that Scripture is inspiring, although it surely is for you and I as well. Inspiration in the Bible means *theopneustos*—literally 'God-breathed.' "

A student in his early twenties raised his hand. He had a stylish haircut and a face of red stubble. "I'm just curious," he said. "We're working towards a proof of the Bible as inspired, and all the evidence we're using is coming from the Bible itself. I'm just curious, because I've heard other people question this approach—and obviously we're not bound by reason, necessarily—but when you're working through a proof scientifically, if you use the thing to prove itself, it doesn't work out rationally. So how would you explain divine inspiration to somebody who questioned it from that perspective?"

Horrell took the question in stride. "I think we'd back up and say, 'Why believe the Bible at all?' And that takes us back to the resurrection, doesn't it? There is a historically verifiable event—as much as anything can be verified—called the resurrection. That proves with ninety-five percent certainty that, given the juridical and historical evidence, Jesus Christ really rose from the dead. The signs and wonders of the early church also put forth evidence, in a scientific way, that what is testified to is truly of God."

"So the proof of inspiration is found outside of Scripture?" asked the student. "There's scientific proof?"

"The scientific proof itself has decomposed. Let's speak of historical truth: as much as something can be proved, the resurrection stands gigantic against the great uniformitarian way of understanding the universe. It stands there as—one cannot say indisputably, but certainly verifiably in a reasonable sense—proof of God, of Christ's sonship, and of the testimony of his followers."

"So faith still comes into it?" asked the student, sounding slightly confused.

"Faith comes in with every aspect of what we're talking about," said Horrell. "But we believe the Old and New Testament are based in history. Judeo-Christianity, particularly Christianity, is the one religion that is rooted in objective evidence."

Theology is what happens when tradition hits a bump in the road. Phrases like *biblical literalism* come into fashion only when people stop taking certain things for granted. The Catholic doctrine of papal infallibility, for example, issued not from the mouth of St. Peter but from the First Vatican Council of 1869, a time when modernity was beginning to challenge the traditional authority of Rome. Before then, Catholics generally assumed that whatever the pope said could be trusted. The same goes for Protestants and the Bible. Just nine years after the First Vatican Council, the Niagara Bible Conference, an important early fundamentalist gathering at Niagara-on-the-Lake, Ontario, adopted one of the first statements on the divine inspiration of Scripture. For centuries, American believers felt no pressing need to defend the Bible. The authority of Scripture was a bedrock reality. By the mid-nineteenth century, those assumptions had begun to change.

After Alexis de Tocqueville completed his tour of the United States in 1832, the French thinker and historian concluded that Americans were the most religious people he had ever encountered. "Upon my arrival in the United States," he wrote, "the religious aspect of the country was the first thing that struck my attention." The firebrand revivalists of the Second Great Awakening had turned upper New York State into "the burned-over district." During the French Revolution, the Church had retreated before the secular armies of the Enlightenment. In the New World, religion and democracy seemed to advance in lockstep. "There is no country in the world," wrote Tocqueville, "where the Christian religion retains a greater influence over the souls of men than in America."[5]

Three decades later, another foreign visitor arrived keen to observe the celebrated American religiosity. John Nelson Darby, a British ex-clergyman and itinerant preacher, stayed for four weeks and traveled two thousand miles, making stops in Detroit, Chicago, St. Louis, and at points along the Mississippi and in New York State. He came to opposite conclusions from Tocqueville.

"The church is more worldly in America than anywhere you would find it . . . inordinately wicked," wrote Darby. While acknowledging "a certain measure of outward evangelical activity," He described the state of religious life as "feebleness itself." In churches, Darby found pulpits occupied by ministers who were "more skeptical than the hearers." Of particular concern was the lack of respect shown to Scripture. Ministers, he noted, no longer made their points by quoting from the Bible. "Scripture has little authority," he wrote. "You must reason about it, or the sermon will not do."[6]

Much in America had changed since Tocqueville's visit. The ardor for revival had cooled, the Civil War was tempering the optimism of the early republic, and industrialization, which had already done so much to transform Europe, was beginning to make its mark on the New World. The secular ideals of the Enlightenment and the scientific revolution were also trickling down to the streets and challenging the cultural monopoly held by Christianity.

These intellectual currents had a profound effect on the study of the Bible. Scholars began to study the Old and New Testaments as historical and cultural documents rather than as revelation. The "higher critics," they were called, and they came to conclusions that flatly contradicted the commonsense beliefs long assumed by Protestants. King David, it turned out, did not write the Psalms; Isaiah had been at least two people; the Gospels were not a stenography of Jesus' words and actions recorded by his disciples but the fanciful reconstruction of later generations. When the higher critics compared the Bible to the sacred writings of other civilizations from the same period, the numerous similarities led them to conclude that the biblical authors had cribbed from their neighbors. Suddenly, the Bible was much more complicated than it seemed, and more fallible than anyone had imagined.

During the seventeenth and eighteenth centuries, the authority of the Bible had so been taken for granted that no American theologian had bothered to work out a systematic defense of divine inspiration and inerrancy. By the mid-nineteenth century, such work became critical. If the Scriptures couldn't be trusted in some areas, how could they be trusted in others? Ministers and evangelists needed a way to reassure believers that the Bible was still the sole reliable path to knowledge of God.

Their solution, biblical literalism, built upon earlier Protestant traditions. Yet it was essentially a new way of reading the Bible that incorporated the ideas of Common Sense Realism, an eighteenth-century philosophical movement that issued from the Scottish Enlightenment. Common Sense Realism taught that reality can be known using a person's inborn rationality and "common sense," an argument that evangelicals modified to assert that any layperson could access the full meaning of Scripture simply by applying common sense to draw out the plain, literal meaning.

The next thing that believers needed was a system of interpretation, one that could compete with the sophistication of higher criticism. That system, known as dispensationalism, sprang from the mind of John Nelson Darby. For a founding father of a populist religious movement, Darby had limitations. He hated large crowds and was incapacitated by stage fright. And while he wrote voluminously—his *Collected Writings* comprises thirty-four volumes—the majority of his works deflect the most patient attempts at comprehension. "He delighted in a concatenated sentence," wrote one friend, "sometimes with parenthesis within parenthesis."[7]

Darby began to develop dispensationalism in the 1830s. It was based on an old idea, the notion that biblical history is divided into discrete epochs or dispensations. Every dispensation followed the same pattern: God would set up the rules of the game, and humans would break them. Whatever configuration was tried, matters degenerated until God was forced to intervene and establish a new dispensation on different terms.

One advantage of Darby's system was that it allowed believers to accept most of what modern reason and science had demonstrated about the universe while affirming the literal truth of the Scriptures. In earlier times, God had frequently intervened in history—parting the Red Sea to free the Israelites, destroying all life on earth with a global flood—but in the current dispensation, known as the Church Age, God had stepped back from the world, allowing it to run according to Newtonian principles. The age of miracles was over. Dispensationalism gave believers a way to reconcile the claims of tradition and modernity.

Another attractive feature of Darby's system was its view of history. Darby believed that history was driven by conflict, a notion shared by most nineteenth-century thinkers. Sigmund Freud, for example, argued that each new generation overthrows the last in a cycle of struggle that recasts the ancient myth of Oedipus. Charles Darwin's theory of natural selection, encapsulated in *The Origin of Species*, enshrined conflict as a science, the key to all biological development. For Karl Marx, the worker's utopia of Communism grew out of the history of class struggle between oppressed and oppressor. Against these secular models of conflict and progress, Darby returned to an earlier conception of history as the outworking of supernatural warfare between God and Satan.

Dispensationalism was an innovative system of interpretation that took verses from all over the Bible and stitched them together into a complex timetable of future events. Few could follow its elaborate twists and turns, so Darby's disciples came up with a series of colorful charts, which were used as teaching aids to drill the basic outline into the proletariat. When Darby said that God was concerned with history, what he really meant was that God *was* history, time impregnated with eternity, event birthing event in an unending golden chain. History rolled its way across the heavens like Ezekiel's chariot, divine causality radiating from every spoke. The mind of God was a machine, and the Bible was the blueprint.

From 1862 to 1877, Darby made seven trips to North America, spending a total of almost seven years in Canada and the United States. His devotion to every word of Scripture endeared him to theological conservatives in Presbyterian, Baptist, and

Methodist congregations who were battling the encroachment of theological liberalism. One year after Darby's death in 1882, dispensationalists began an annual Bible conference in Niagara-on-the-Lake, Ontario, which focused on reading the Bible, especially its prophetic books, in a "plain manner." The conference members drew up a fourteen-point creed, beginning with a bold statement on divine inspiration, which was later adopted into the constitutions of many fundamentalist churches.

One conference participant thought up a better way to spread the "lost truths" of literalism and dispensationalism to the common man. Cyrus I. Scofield, a Congregational minister based in Dallas, Texas, asked his wife to cut up two King James Bibles, pasting each page on a larger sheet of paper. In the widened margins, he assembled a chain of footnotes and cross-references that made it easy for believers to follow the dispensational system. His annotations were like a scaffolding erected around a grand old building in need of repair, except that, in this case, all of the work went into the scaffolding instead of the structure. Scofield's fearful system of notes and cross-references gave some bystanders the impression of a serious conservation effort; as others observed, it also obstructed large parts of the Bible from view.

In 1909, Oxford University Press published the *Scofield Reference Bible*, which went on to sell more than 20 million copies and become the most influential work in the history of fundamentalism. One prominent fundamentalist offered this endorsement: "From a position of entire ignorance of the Scriptures to a position of oracular religious certainty . . . for some people requires from three to six months with a Scofield Bible."[8] Dispensationalism promised the unadulterated essence of the

Word delivered to your doorstep with a minimum of struggle or effort.

By the end of the twentieth century, Darby's disciples largely controlled fundamentalism. Every major American revivalist since Dwight L. Moody has been a dispensationalist. Televangelists such as Pat Robertson, James Dobson, Jerry Falwell, and James Hagee embraced the system, as did such bestselling fundamentalist authors as Hal Lindsey (*The Late Great Planet Earth*) and Tim LaHaye (the *Left Behind* series). For millions of believers, dispensationalism became synonymous with biblical literalism.

Part of the genius of dispensationalism is that its imprint, while ubiquitous, is also anonymous. Most rank-and-file fundamentalists have never heard of Darby. His ideas affect believers subconsciously, running in the background like a computer's operating system. It succeeds by becoming invisible, convincing believers that they are simply encountering the plain, unfiltered meaning of the Bible.

In their eagerness to do battle against false gods, literalists such as Darby and Scofield created their own golden calf. Matthew St. John is the pastor of Dallas's Scofield Memorial Church, once the home pulpit of the man behind the *Scofield Reference Bible*. St. John resembles a retired college quarterback, the kind of guy who can disarm an audience with a big smile and a playful wink. He describes himself as a dispensationalist but admits that the system has tempted many into a form of biblical idolatry. "I think in fundamentalism there has been a tendency to nearly worship the Scriptures," he said. "Nobody would ever say that, of course. And I don't know that anybody intends that, but it kind of happens. I'm talking about folk that, despite their good intentions, end up valuing the written Word more than the Living Word. As a result, they may know everything there is to know about Scripture, but they're not loving their wives, they're not building up their kids, they could care less for their neighbor. Frankly, I think that's more commonplace than we want to admit."

The best legacy of literalism is that it helped to reassure millions of believers that the Bible could be relied upon at a time when Western progress threatened to make it irrelevant. Just as important, it allowed them to continue to follow a lifestyle of devotion based on the Reformation principle of *sola scriptura*— the notion that the Scriptures are the sole authority in Christian life. But as always, there were unintended consequences. While resisting rationalist attacks on the Bible, literalism made fundamentalists into a mirror image of the enemy. The dispensational system turned religion into a mental exercise and hid the Bible's strange riches behind a screen of notes and cross-references. Fundamentalism became a branch of Gnosticism, the ancient Christian heresy that argued that people are saved by a secret form of knowledge rather than through a relationship with a living savior. Literalism had mapped the mind of God, but missed the beating heart.

For the past eighty years, dispensationalism has been synonymous with fundamentalism at Dallas Theological Seminary. Recent indications, however, suggest that Dallas is moving away from its historical roots. Increasingly, believers are choosing to encounter the grand old edifice of Scripture without Darby's help.

In late October, Dallas Seminary hosts Fall Fest on the manicured main quad of its campus. The festival is a big event on the social calendar, a chance for students and faculty to mix outside class. In 2006, a few hundred people mingled on the grass while Christian rock reverberated loudly among the buildings. Students queued with softballs to try their luck at dropping a favorite professor in the dunk tank. In the days leading up to the event, student organizers left a number of playful chalk messages on campus sidewalks. "Come out and find a wife!" read one of them. A few took offense. The following day, the message had been scrubbed away.

One student who enjoyed the joke was Ross, a single guy in his mid-twenties with a groomed pad of stubble on his chin. Before coming to Dallas, Ross earned an undergraduate degree in finance and spent two years as an evangelist in Slovakia. When he arrived on campus, Ross had never heard of dispensationalism; two years later, he still didn't know what to think. "I probably agree with it," he said, shrugging noncommittally. "I want to learn more about it first." His friends were even less convinced. Dispensationalism was "too rigid," they said. "It doesn't allow you to figure things out for yourself."

While many seminarians now regard Darby as too frosty and cerebral, the Dallas administration is steering away from its hardline past in the direction of mainstream evangelicalism. The course calendar emphasizes evangelism and spiritual development, with fewer offerings in classic dispensational topics such as prophecy. Dallas faculty are also wavering in their support. "I don't know of a current scholar—a real scholar—who is defending the system," said John Hannah, the Dallas professor in church history.

Ross told me a story from one of his own classes, in which the professor led a discussion about the relative importance of various doctrines. "You have to be willing to ask yourself what you're willing to die for," the professor said. "The virgin birth, the resurrection, the inerrancy of Scripture—I'm willing to die for that. I wouldn't die for dispensationalism."

A good part of the damage done to dispensationalism has been self-inflicted. During the second half of the twentieth century, fundamentalist scholars demonstrated the same flair for schism that paralyzed international socialism, splintering into "classic," "revised," and "progressive" wings. Arguments over how the seven-year Tribulation period relates to the timing of the Rapture (scholars carefully staked out "pre-," "mid-," and "post-Tribulation" positions, as well as something known as "pre-Wrath") have also fed internal divisions. Faced with such a profusion of choices, many rank-and-file believers simply don't know what to believe.

Even in stalwart fundamentalist churches such as Scofield Memorial, dispensationalism is becoming an issue of "don't ask, don't tell." According to St. John, when new interns arrive at his church from Dallas Theological Seminary, the first question they ask is, how important is dispensationalism? "I tell them, 'Probably nobody will ever ask you about it, because most folks really don't care,'" he said. "People aren't arguing whether King David really lived or not. They're trying to figure out how to talk to their granddaughter who's dating a Muslim. They're trying to figure out how to have a good attitude with their boss, who's a pain in the rear. The conversation has just changed. We've moved on to a new conflict. The arguments now are about authenticity. People want to know God in an intimate way and not just be lectured at. They want to *know* him."

What effect do these changes have on how fundamentalists

read the Bible? For a handful of biblical scholars at places like Dallas Theological Seminary, the decline of dispensationalism has produced a moment of quiet crisis. "For the first time in a century," said Hannah, "we have no idea what we mean by literalism."

For the vast majority of believers, however, life goes on. No matter how muddled their attempts to define the nature of divine inspiration or to explain how the Bible can present a flat-earth cosmology and yet remain free of error, fundamentalists will continue to seek a private audience with the Almighty in the written Word, to beg a little light amid the darkness of daily life. As tradition instructs, they will carry out daily rituals of reading, hearing, and proclaiming the Word, hoping to pass beyond the black curtain of type and prostrate their hearts before the holy. The key to literalism, it turns out, abides not in its ability to deliver the plain, commonsense meaning of the Bible—a book whose powers are protean—but in how it protects a Protestant culture of ritual devotion built around the worship of the Word, a way of life that will continue long after the charms of literalism have been exhausted.

Chapter 3

SAVED

THE PSALMS SPEAK of what a poet later called "the hound of heaven"—a love so dogged that it pursues men and women to the ends of the earth. Psalm 139 asks, "Where can I go from your spirit? Or where can I flee from your presence? If I ascend to heaven, you are there; if I make my bed in Sheol, you are there. If I take the wings of the morning and settle at the farthest limits of the sea, even there your hand shall lead me, and your right hand shall hold me fast."

I'd like to think that God paid me that kind of attention. The truth was, I didn't need it. I had my maternal grandmother. Though she never preached a sermon in her life, my grandmother was the most relentless evangelist I ever met. She stuffed her purse with gospel tracts and pressed them on strangers like breath mints. At the edge of her property, she put up a massive green sign that said, "What think ye of Christ?" I thought the choice of verse a little indirect for her methods. "I don't want to be pushy," she said. "I just want to make people think."

She was a paradigm of Brethren femininity: frugal yet generous, pretty yet unadorned, fervent in her love for the Lord. She kept her hair uncut, as the apostle Paul prescribed, and always took notes during the gospel meeting. To survive the tedium of a dull preacher, believers developed a range of techniques to feign attention—squinting or pouting, while raising a hand to the jaw—even as they thought about having the tires rotated on the Buick. Your mind couldn't wander if you were taking notes.

She loved to tell the story of how she got saved. In her early twenties, she had been in a car accident, which shook her awake to a vital ingredient missing from her life. She looked for something to fill the hole, but the churches she visited felt like social clubs. The ministers were bemused by her earnest questions about sin and hell. When she heard that a distant relative had gotten born again, she paid him a visit.

"That's when I knew I wanted it," she said. "That's what I called it—*it*."

Each night, after the kids were in bed, she sat with her husband at the kitchen table reading the Bible, trying to figure out how to get saved. One evening, they read the third chapter of the Gospel of John: "The wind bloweth where it listeth, and thou hearest the sound thereof, but canst not tell when it cometh, and whither it goeth: so is every one that is born of the Spirit."

She had no idea what it meant. She just knew she believed it. In a flash, everything changed. The world was bathed in light. She told her husband what had happened. "You're just worked up," he said. "Go make us a cup of tea. We'll see how you feel about it in the morning." The next morning, she felt just the same—reborn, a new creature. She was twenty-five.

The next day, she went to her parents and told them she'd found a peace she'd never known before. She wanted them to come with her to the Gospel Hall on Sunday night and refused to take no for an answer. On Monday, she started badgering again.

At first, the family was amused by her enthusiasm, figuring that in a few weeks she'd be on to something else. After a month, they begged her for a moment's peace. When she dropped by for a visit her sister locked herself in the bathroom.

Eventually, my grandmother's persistence was rewarded. First her siblings came to the Lord—all seven of them. Then her parents. Her four daughters were swaddled in the gospel and raised in the fear and admonition of the Lord. No dances, no dating, no makeup, no wearing pants. They were not to use immodest words such as *armpit* or *belly button*. One after another, my mother and her sisters fell like dominoes. When grandchildren came along, she turned her prodigious gifts on us.

Her ambitions for me were always clear. It didn't really matter what I did in this life, so long as I accepted Christ as my savior. When I slept over at the farm, she would kneel beside my bed and pray the Lord to plant a hunger in my heart for the gospel. If I missed gospel meeting on Sunday night, I'd get a phone call a few hours later. "I didn't see you out," she'd say. "Are you sick?" Each year on my birthday, I opened my grandmother's card and feigned surprise when a gospel tract fell out. After my brother got his first car, she hid tracts in the glove box, like clues in an Easter egg hunt.

She picked the tracts that she thought we'd find the most interesting. Usually they opened with an adventure story or tale of disaster. I remember one about a submarine. It was 1939, and the newest sub in the American fleet was stricken by a mechanical failure. The captain ordered the flooded engine room sealed off.

Just in time, a sailor managed to swing shut the large steel door, saving the lives of thirty-three men but dooming his best friend, who was on the wrong side. Then the subtle allegory was revealed. The stricken vessel was the world, sunk in sin. Rather than see humanity perish, God had provided a way to be saved, but the door of salvation would soon be forever shut.

My grandfather was saved a week after my grandmother, while praying alone in his bedroom. One day, he showed me where it happened. The house still stands on a corner of the farm that looks out over fallow hayfields, but the room itself is gone, the walls knocked down to create a workshop. Power cords snaked through piles of sawdust on the floor. A smell of moldering wallpaper hung in the air. He took my arm and led me to a spot where the sawdust had carefully been swept away. There was a large circle on the floor, drawn in in pencil, with an X running through the middle. "God touched me there," he said.

Like all Protestants, fundamentalists trace their roots to the Reformation, the sixteenth-century movement that began as an attempt to save the Church from corruption but resulted in the breakup of Western Christendom. As a historical event, the Reformation had numerous causes—religious, political, social, economic. But in the sacred memory of Protestants, it is the story of one man's conversion to God. For much of his youth, Martin Luther was beset by what might today be called an existential crisis. As a monk, he struggled for relief from the feeling that he was a guilty sinner going to hell. Nothing could quiet his anxious soul. He tried every rite of penance he could find, even sleeping outside in the snow. Sometimes after confessing his sins, he immediately returned to the confessional with fresh ones to confess.

One night in 1519, while Luther was in the tower library of his German monastery reading Paul's Letter to the Romans, he was smitten by a sudden realization: rather than try to make himself righteous before God, he would surrender himself to grace, the divine righteousness of the cross. "All at once," he wrote, "I felt that I had been born again and entered into paradise itself through open gates." The experience became the foundation for Luther's doctrine of "salvation by grace through faith," the intellectual cornerstone of the Reformation and, for many Protestants, a concise way to separate Protestants from Catholics.

Luther didn't write an account of his conversion until twenty-five years later and then saw fit to do so only in a preface that accompanied a translation of his Latin writings. Yet, the story acquired a powerful charge among English and then American evangelicals. In mid-eighteenth-century Connecticut, David Brainerd, a Puritan missionary, described his conversion similarly as a return to paradise. "I felt myself in a new world," he wrote, "and everything about me appeared with a different aspect from what it was wont to do."[1] John Wesley, the founder of Methodism, owed an even greater debt to Luther. On May 24, 1738, Wesley was listening to a reading of Luther's preface to Paul's Letter to the Romans when he felt his heart "strangely warmed." The story is a marvelous example of telescopic narrative. Like a set of Russian dolls, it breaks apart to reveal two more—Luther and Paul—nested inside.

The fact that both Wesley and Luther cite Paul in their testimonies of faith is no coincidence. No other conversion narrative generates the same respect among Protestants. As Homer's *Iliad* and *Odyssey* established the pattern for every Hollywood adventure film, among the 46 percent of Americans who claim to have "had a born-again experience with Jesus Christ," it is common to talk of "seeing the light" or having had a "Damascus road experience."

It's a simple tale, told by the apostle himself in the Letter to Galatians and secondhand in the Acts of the Apostles. Paul, then known as Saul, was a notorious persecutor of the Jewish followers of Jesus. While on his way to Damascus, he was suddenly surrounded by a blinding light. A loud voice thundered, "Saul, why are you persecuting me?" Saul fell to the ground and asked who was speaking. The voice replied that it was Jesus and told Paul to go into Damascus, where he would receive further instructions. Blinded, Paul was led by his companions into the city, where a holy man restored his sight and told him that his destiny was to become a missionary for the gospel.

Though they range across eighteen centuries, the conversion stories of Paul, Luther, and Wesley share remarkable similarities. In each case, a man finds salvation in the sudden. Each tale identifies the precise point of transformation, pegging it to a moment in time and space. God always addresses the soul directly, through either speech or the written word.

In spite of these shared qualities, Paul's tale has significant differences. Nowhere does the apostle communicate any sense of inner turmoil or guilt. Neither does he make any show of repentance, a critical step in any Protestant model of conversion. As biblical scholar Krister Stendahl points out, Paul's Damascus

Road encounter has less in common with modern assumptions about conversion than it does with ancient patterns in the Old Testament that dictated how God called a prophet. The poster child of Protestant conversion would have a hard time recognizing the American conversion industry, with its busy altar calls and tearful confessions.

Over the last five centuries, what it means to "get saved" has gone through its own dramatic process of transformation. Modern conversion, with its promises of instant gratification, quick fixes, and assembly-line authenticity, may owe its greatest debt not to Paul but to secular American culture.

Conversion goes by many names: getting saved, being born again, knowing your sins forgiven, being justified by grace through faith, getting washed in the blood of the Lamb, settling the debt, finding blessed assurance, having your name written in the Lamb's Book of Life, being baptized in the spirit, knowing the Lord, getting right with God, receiving the gift of personal salvation. The etymological root of conversion is "to turn." This turning operates in two senses: the sinner turns away from his old ways and turns toward a new, enlightened form of being—from darkness to light, ignorance to knowledge, corruption to purity, guilt to innocence, flesh to spirit. One could see the Bible as one long story about the turning of the human race back to God after going its own way in the Garden of Eden. "Turn us again, O God," writes the Psalmist, "and cause thy face to shine, and we shall be saved." His laments provide a key to the psychology of the convert—as one scholar puts it, "sighing, groaning, despairing, sure that God has hidden His face, spending nights in sleepless agony, tossing wearily to and fro, watering the couch with tears."[2]

In the Old Testament, conversion is corporate, focused on the nation of Israel as a whole. In the New Testament, the circle expands from Jews to gentiles, even as the club gets more exclusive. "For many are called, but few are chosen," Jesus said. Thousands come to hear him speak, but only a dozen become disciples. Much attention is paid to the moment of salvation. In 1 Peter, it is a calling out of darkness into light. In 2 Corinthians, Paul describes the convert as a "new creature"; in Romans, he says the believer must undergo a spiritual death so that he may rise again. But the primary metaphor of evangelical conversion comes in the third chapter of John's Gospel, where Jesus likens it to the experience of birth: "Except a man be born again, he cannot enter the kingdom of God."

Though the Brethren believed that all Scripture was fuel for the soul, the third chapter of John held pride of place in the orbits of biblical wisdom. Any seeker who relied on its constellation of thirty-six verses and the heart's inner compass could chart a course for the harbors of eternal peace. In a pinch, all you really needed was the sixteenth verse: "For God so loved the world that he gave his only begotten Son, that whosoever believeth in him should not perish, but have everlasting life." John 3:16 has forever been the sum of evangelical theology, the polestar of Scripture. "It's plain and clear," my grandmother said. "It's the simplest verse in the Bible. If you can understand that, you've got it."

It was so simple a child could grasp it. All you had to do was ask the Lord Jesus Christ into your heart and you would be saved. Some Brethren put it more pithily: "Only believe."

There was nothing to do—all the doing had been done. But what exactly did you have to believe? That men and women are born in sin and universally destined for hell. That God in his mercy sent his son to take upon himself, through death on the cross, the punishment incurred by Adam's sin. If you could swallow this précis of the human condition, you were ready to be forgiven.

Like any good Brethren, my grandmother looked to Damascus Road as her model. Her salvation had been sudden, instantaneous, and total in its effect. But when she shared the mechanics with me, it sounded anything but simple. There were preparatory steps. First, you had to recognize that you were a lost sinner and needed salvation. This was often the greatest hurdle. What Harriet Tubman said of slavery—"If I could have convinced more slaves that they were slaves, I would have freed thousands more"—was also true of sin. As my grandfather the preacher liked to say, "Getting people saved is easy. It's getting them lost that's the hard part."

But even if a soul got good and lost, there was no guarantee it would find its way home again. Some would wait weeks or months before taking the next step. The more anxiety a person demonstrated, the greater the sign of the Spirit's striving. God was trying to get your attention. In gospel meeting I often felt the preacher was interpreting my facial expression as a sign of whether the Spirit was striving with me.

Once the Spirit plowed the soil, planting could begin. Jesus didn't want winners. You had to believe you were a worm. The trick was to take the general formula—Jesus died for the sins of the world—and make it personal—Jesus died for me. A popular technique was to insert your name into John 3:16. "Put your name in there!" my grandfather said. "For God so loved *you* that he gave his only begotten son that *you* might not perish . . ."

I tried this strategy often as a boy of ten or eleven, but I could never get the engine to turn over. I'd reach the end of the verse and wait for some kind of message—a strange tingling or a light or a rush of mental clarity. Nothing. What did it feel like to have your sins forgiven? I wondered. Was it even a feeling? When I asked my grandmother, she warned me that emotions could easily lead a person astray. "Feelings come and go," she said.

"So does it happen in your head?" I asked.

"Well, it's not head knowledge, but your head is involved. It's in your heart."

Okay, I thought. It takes place in your heart, but it's not a feeling. It has something to do with your head, but it isn't knowledge. If getting lost was the hard part, I was doing a fantastic job.

I turned to Paul for consolation. He didn't help. His story was too perfect. How could I hope to replicate it? No voice had ever thundered at me from heaven. Even my sins—lying to my parents, stealing candy from the corner store—seemed paltry. I'd thrown a few rocks at windows, but I'd never stoned anybody. If I was unimpressive as a sinner, how could I hope to impress as a saint?

My grandmother said that to get saved you had to want it more than anything else in the world, even if only for a few seconds. "Seek ye first the kingdom of God," the Bible said, "and all these things shall be added unto you." I had to want it more than chocolate and tree forts, more than Christmas and my birthday combined. I tried to clear the clutter from my heart, to pile it in a closet somewhere, but I could never quite get the door to close. There were too many things that I wanted.

Even if I had been able to clear my mind and will one thing, there was still the dicey issue of free will itself. As in, did it exist? The Brethren were old-fashioned Calvinists who taught that God had predestined certain souls to heaven and others to hell. This presented a problem. If my cards had already been dealt, what could I do to change them?

I put the question to my grandmother. She frowned with impatience, as though I'd asked her what color my hair was. "God sees everything," she said, "so he already knows what you're going to choose. He knows whether you're going to choose heaven." I still wasn't getting it, so she continued. "It's like two tracks of a railroad," she said, holding her arms out to illustrate. Human free will and predestination ran in parallel lines. The Gordian knot had neatly been severed.

From my confused expression, she must have thought the Spirit was striving mightily with me, because a few days later she showed up at the house with a preacher in tow. He carried a leather Bible bag with his initials branded on the side. She left us alone, and we sat at the kitchen table and read over a few verses. He ran through the ABC checklist: acknowledge that you're a sinner, believe that Jesus paid the price for your sins, and commit your life to Jesus. I promised to think about it and to keep reading and praying, but in my heart I already felt powerless to change my fate. The Spirit no longer strove with me. I was damned.

No Protestant group cared about conversion as much as the Puritans. In America, church membership in the Massachusetts Bay Colony required applicants to submit a spiritual autobiography describing their experience of "saving grace"—something neither Luther nor Calvin asked of their followers. Then again, few Protestants in continental Europe could imagine the conditions under which the Puritans had arrived in the New World: the ordeal of the Atlantic crossing, a collective baptism of death and rebirth. Those who survived (one in five died of shipwreck, starvation, or sickness) used the story of Exodus to make sense of their experience. They had escaped the chains of the English pharaoh, crossed the Red Sea, and entered the Promised Land. This New World required a New Man. Joseph Alleine, an eighteenth-century Puritan, wrote, "Conversion is not the putting in a patch of holiness; but with the true convert holiness is woven into all his powers, principles, and practice. The sincere Christian is quite a new fabric, from the foundation to the top-stone. He is a new man, a new creature."[3]

In *The Moon and Sixpence*, W. Somerset Maugham justified the rich variety of Christian conversion as the expressions of individual need. "Conversion," he wrote, "may come under many shapes, and it may be brought about in many ways. With some men it needs a cataclysm, as a stone may be broken to fragments by the fury of a torrent; but with some it comes gradually, as a stone may be worn away by the ceaseless fall of a drop of water."[4] In the turbulent days of the Reformation, few held such a laissez-faire attitude to the divine economy. Though all reformers defended the necessity of personal conversion, they were deeply divided over whether the experience was slow or sudden. Heinrich Bullinger, a sixteenth-century Swiss reformer, rejected Paul's Damascus experience as the prototype of Christian conversion. Salvation, he said, was a prolonged courtship in which the sinner prepared the heart to receive divine grace through introspection and meditation.[5] Bullinger's Swiss compatriot Huldrych

Zwingli, and William Tyndale, an early translator of the Bible into English, took the opposite view. Every act of salvation, they said, was Pauline: divine grace smote the soul of the sinner like a hammer on an anvil. "The Word of God is so sure and strong," Zwingli wrote, "that if God wills, all things are done the moment that he speaks his Word."[6]

Surprisingly, English and American Puritans sided with Bullinger, opting for what was called the preparation model over the ideal of instant catharsis. Throughout the seventeenth century, Puritan divines cataloged emotional states and psychological symptoms in an elaborate morphology of salvation, anticipating the inward turn of modern psychoanalysis. As one scholar put it, it was "the Reformation turned back on itself." The Puritans made their hearts into laboratories, studying each subtle shift in feeling or mood with the precision that the Renaissance had brought to human anatomy and the physical universe.

One discovery the Puritans made was that the second birth had a surprisingly long gestation period. William Perkins identified no less than ten stages in a typical case of "saving grace." First of all, a sinner was wrenched from complacency, often though a close brush with death. This was necessary, he wrote, "to breake and subdue the stubbornness of our nature." Newly awakened to his mortality, the sinner then read or heard the Word of God to become aware of "his own peculiar and proper sins." Self-knowledge led to the next stage—"conviction" or "humiliation"—in which the soul was gripped by "legall feare" and fell into despair. Despair eventually gave way to a "will and desire to believe," a small seed of faith planted in the heart by God himself. Yet, as soon as hope returned, the sinner was plunged back into darkness, to struggle with the demons of doubt and despair.[7]

For those who suffered persecution in England for preaching the "new birth," the New World offered freedom of worship. Yet, in a perverse twist, the Calvinist theology for which they died denied them the smallest freedom in determining the fate of their own souls. Because the Lord's ways were mysterious, no one could know for sure whether a conversion was authentic or simply a product of wishful thinking. "Certainty," knowing that God was with you, was deemed the opposite of "security," a sign of complacency and delusion: the man most secure of his salvation was paradoxically the one least likely to be saved. The faithful clung to fear and doubt as faint signs that God had not given up striving with their souls. Hope lay in the promise of anguished lifetime introspection. The elect looked forward to an endless succession of bright mountaintops and dark valleys. The only rest from spiritual combat was the grave.

The Puritans provided the seed of the evangelical obsession with "saving grace"; the Great Awakening yielded its first plentiful harvest. During the 1730s, religious revivals crisscrossed the American colonies. On the steps in front of Philadelphia's courthouse, seventy-eight thousand people gathered to hear the famed English evangelist George Whitefield preach the call to conversion. Wherever he went, Whitefield taught Paul's Damascus road experience as the essential pattern for every new convert to the faith. Preaching in Glasgow in 1741, Whitefield said, "Ah my dear friends, this must be done to you as well as to Saul . . . God must speak to you by Name, God must reach your Heart in particular, ye must be brought to see the Evil of Sin, and cry out after Jesus Christ."[8]

While older Puritans welcomed these testimonies of rebirth, the "bodily effects" that often accompanied them—sudden outbursts, convulsions, or fainting spells—were denounced as demonic. The most articulate defender of the new revivals and its surprising side effects was Jonathan Edwards. An accomplished scientist, he found nothing in the natural world to compare with the spontaneous outpourings of the Holy Spirit: "I am bold to say," wrote Edwards, "that the work of God in the conversion of one soul . . . is a more glorious work of God than the creation of the whole material universe."[9]

Though Edwards championed the new model of sudden conversion, he continued to view humans as entirely passive recipients of grace. Salvation was "a surprising work of God." John Wesley, the eighteenth-century Anglican minister and founder of Methodism, disagreed. Building on the work of the Dutch reformer Arminius, Wesley turned back the iron jaws of predestination. Fate, Wesley said, was what you make. Every soul could choose heaven. Wesley's theology of free will matched the spirit of postrevolutionary America, where a popular uprising had defeated a king and installed a democratic government based upon the rights and freedoms of the individual. During the Second Great Awakening, in the 1830s, the Methodist Church mobilized armies of lay preachers and circuit riders, many illiterate, who carried to the expanding American frontier the message that "God willeth all men to be saved." A marginal player at the turn of the nineteenth century, by 1850 Methodism was the largest denomination in the country, claiming one third of Americans.

The final step in modernizing American conversion—from anxious, lifelong ordeal to instant, self-willed transformation—came from Charles Grandison Finney, a revivalist from Connecticut. Like Wesley, Finney did not conceive of salvation in dramatic terms, but as a simple calculated decision. "On a Sabbath evening in the autumn of 1821, I made up my mind that I would settle the question of my soul's salvation at once," he wrote.[10] The choice may have held cosmic significance, but the decision itself became almost routine, like buying a pair of shoes.

Finney applied his sensible mind to the methods of religious revival and spotted a number of inefficiencies. Rather than wait for the Spirit to move, he argued that the second birth could be induced at will. Finney introduced a series of "new measures" aimed at streamlining conversion and increasing the yield of souls at each service. He published "how-to" manuals for preachers, pioneering practices such as the altar call and the "anxious bench," where malefactors worked out their salvation in fear and trembling under the guiding hand of a trained professional. At the same time that the industrial revolution was beginning to transform the American countryside, Finney revolutionized the inner landscape of religious experience, eliminating the disorder, inefficiency, and mystery of the divine economy. In return for a simple yes for Jesus, his new measures turned out converts like widgets.

Personal salvation is the American dream. It is the promise of a second chance, of getting something for nothing. The hope of sudden transformation is what drives middle-aged women to feed bags of quarters into slots in Vegas or to go under the blade in Beverly Hills. It fuels the midnight urge to dial the toll-free number at the bottom of your screen. The dream of the fresh start, the perfect getaway, arises from the belief that we can and must be born again, through a process that requires no tangible sacrifice and takes no longer than a Botox injection.

Fundamentalists blame the entertainment industry for breeding a culture of selfishness and entitlement, where personal choice is worshipped. But those same messages can be found in modern notions of conversion. Rather than see salvation in the sum of a person's life, it focuses on a split-second transaction in which an eternity of bliss is exchanged for a onetime commitment, a simple mental act. It's fast-food religion.

A case in point is Hell House, a haunted house–style attraction run by fundamentalist church groups in the days leading up to Halloween. Visitors are led through a series of rooms in which actors dramatize the dangers of ungodly behavior and the torment that awaits sinners in hell. Keenan Roberts, an Assemblies of God pastor in Thornton, Colorado, sells Hell House kits through his church, New Destiny Christian Center, for $299 (the kits include a how-to DVD and a sound track of special effects). Keenan is a spiritual descendant of Finney and his "new measures," going so far as to boast that churches that host their own Hell House can expect a conversion rate of 25 percent. Sinners go in as base material, travel from room to room as on a conveyor belt, and come out as believers.

On the night of Friday the thirteenth, three hundred people queued along the edge of a football field behind Trinity Church of Cedar Hill, Texas, for the opening night of Hell House. Most were teenagers, though a number of parents chaperoned younger children. A fast-food truck did brisk business in hot dogs and nachos. Thirty feet away, an SUV played Christian rock at a deafening volume. The spill-off from the stadium lights suffused the crowd with bleached tones.

By 2007, Trinity had hosted Hell House sixteen times, making it one of the oldest in the country, as well as one of the most popular, drawing an average of ten thousand visitors each season. In 2001, a documentary was made about the production that brought attacks from local community leaders, as well as a crush of new fans. Among them were Rosie, a short, recently divorced Latina in her early thirties, and her hyperactive thirteen-year-old son, Tommy. This was their second Hell House, and Rosie had volunteered to work the "prayer room," Hell House's version of an altar call. A few years ago, their lives had been very different. "I was a total partier," she said. After the dissolution of Rosie's marriage, she became restless and unhappy. A friend invited her to Trinity, where she gave her life to Jesus. Tommy followed and immediately began to evangelize his friends. Last year, he brought his best friend to Hell House. "I just *had* to get him *saved*," he said, shaking his head.

The line moved slowly. Every ten or fifteen minutes, a black Chevy pickup with tinted windows arrived pulling a long trailer lined with hay. Thirty new passengers piled onto the trailer and the truck sped off into the field, disappearing into a dark ring of trees behind the football stadium. After waiting almost two hours, our turn came. We climbed into the trailer and rode the hay bales to a set of connected house trailers in the woods.

In room after room, short skits depicted the results of the seven deadly sins, redacted down to three: sex, stimulants, and Satan worship. One skit, set in a nightclub, addressed the dangers of drinking. The young actors seemed to relish the opportunity to enact such forbidden pleasures as close dancing and intoxication. Other scenes dealt with the perils of telephone psychics and premarital sex. Audience reactions varied by age and gender. The preteens stuck by their mothers for protection; the teenagers were cool and standoffish. One boy in baggy, low-riding pants responded to every scene with the same mute glare. The girls were more engaged, taunting the demon-masked actors or laughing at the maudlin dramas.

In Heaven, a largely empty room bestrewn with white sheets, three large plasma-screen TVs depicted a world of angels and domed Byzantine cathedrals. Hell, the dramatic climax of the play, recycled every cliché from popular culture. Arms grasped at visitors through holes in the walls and figures in rags dragged their chains across the floor. A long-haired devil ran about spewing Latin-scented gibberish, causing the boy in the baggy pants to lose his cool. "Get back from me in the name of Jesus!" he shrieked. "You got nothing on me. You have no power over me. Jesus owns me." Beside him, a young mother raised her hand and backed against the wall, using the other arm to shield her ten-year-old son. "Get back in the name of Jesus," she said quietly over and over.

The final room was bare and lit with fluorescent lights. A middle-aged black man and a twentysomething white woman, both in street clothes, stood in silence with their arms crossed. The air was heavy with perspiration. The woman spoke first. She hoped everyone had enjoyed the play. Everything we had seen, she said, was based on real events, events that were chosen because they carried an important message: that anyone who did not have a personal relationship with Jesus Christ would be susceptible to the same evils that befell the characters.

The teens, who had at first been respectful and attentive, grew restless. A cell phone chimed. A girl answered and started up a conversation. "Can I get you to take that outside?" the woman

asked. The world was full of demons, she said. They sought to influence our decisions, to steer us away from God. Another phone
rang. The kid in the baggy pants went to answer, but the older
man stopped him.

"Excuse me," the man said, "but I've got something to say.
You all might think this is funny, but I assure you this is no joke.
You want to talk about demons? Try this: There are demons. In
this room. Right now. At this very moment. They'll do everything they can to distract you, or to use somebody else to distract
you. So you can sit back and blow this off. You can say, 'They
don't know what they're talking about.' But it is happening. You
can't change that. You have to make a decision right now
whether you want to shut out that distraction or give in to it.
Because they're smart. They know they've only got so much
time to do their work. So right now, you got to decide. Which is
it going to be? There are people waiting in the next room to pray
with you if you need somebody to pray with you. We don't
make no judgments about you if you stay, but know that this is
your chance."

He opened a door leading into darkness. "I'm going to count
to ten. When I'm done, that door is going to close."

He started to count. "Ten . . . Nine . . ." Five or six kids ran
immediately for the door. The tension was palpable. The baggy-
pants kid stared stone-faced at the floor. At three, the man
paused. "Don't look around you at what the person next to you
is doing. Don't let them pull you down with them. If you need
help, you better take it right now, 'cause that door is going to
close."

More young bodies fled through the door, including baggy
pants. Only a handful remained.

"Two . . . One . . . Last chance," the man said. The door shut.

After a heavy pause, the woman spoke again. "If you're still in this room, it's for one of two reasons. Either you've already made your peace with God, or else you aren't being honest with yourself. We're not here to make that judgment. But I hope you remember what you've seen tonight." With that, the door opened again and we were quickly ushered through the darkened prayer room and on to the exit. I caught a fleeting glimpse of shadowed bodies huddled and murmuring together, wrapped in the plaintive folds of prayer. Then we passed the last threshold and broke back into the world, breathing the cool night air and blinking in the false dawn of stadium floodlights.

Where I come from, how you got saved had a lot to do with when you got saved. It was like wisdom teeth. The longer you waited to have them out, the more painful and dramatic the procedure.

Childhood conversions are peaceful, plotless affairs. They accompany the first pangs of conscience, when the will is easiest to mold. It usually starts with a parent or Sunday school teacher explaining how Jesus loves you and wants you to love him too. If the child shows some understanding, he'll sometimes be encouraged to recite a formula that asks Jesus to come and live in his heart. The advantage of a childhood conversion is that it gets the messy business out of the way early. On the downside, some might question a child's testimony as he gets older, on the grounds that he was too young to understand what he was doing.

Adult converts always had the best stories. Usually they'd done something really bad in their former lives: they were alcoholics, divorcées, Catholics. One of my favorites was Dave, a turnip-shaped Buddy Holly with wiry brown hair and heavy-framed glasses that always seemed about to slip off the end of his nose. My brother and I loved when he took the pulpit. The trick to sharing your testimony was giving enough juicy details about your past while denying that you took any enjoyment in it. Dave knew how to wag his head (slowly, wistfully, slightly angled to the rest of the body) as he recalled wild nights of drinking and drug abuse. Dave's Damascus involved a road trip with his buddies in a VW microbus, which careened off the road into a ditch. "The fellow behind the wheel had too much liquid in him," he said. Dave was thrown out of the car but miraculously survived. He said it was the best thing that ever happened to him.

The problem with teenage converts is the high rate of recidivism. In adolescence, the self is never more internally divided, flesh and spirit set in mortal combat. It makes for great drama. After getting saved, it's common to feel a mild euphoria, but a few weeks later, the smiles turn to fretful frowns. Was it real? Did I do it right? Am I fooling myself? Anxiety leads to despair, and the quest for catharsis begins anew. After a while, the heart begins to feel like a lump of overworked dough. No matter how hot the oven, it just won't rise.

Heidegger said there are three states in which humans encounter the greatness of being: joy, despair, and boredom. In the Brethren, I knew little joy—that was supposed to be the reserve of the elect. I also failed to capitalize on my despair. So it was my lot to meet the Lord in my sheer crushing boredom.

I was thirteen. It was a season of change. Old things were passing away. Puberty robbed my face of baby fat and gave me new appetites and a million distractions. My grandmother feared hope would soon be lost. She redoubled her efforts. Tracts flew out of her purse like confetti at a wedding.

One night, when my parents were out of town, I stayed the night with my grandparents. It was a Tuesday, which meant Bible reading, the Brethren meeting held one night a week where men jousted over the meaning of God's Word. The talk was tedious, one brother upbraiding another for mistaking the symbolism of the golden breastplate of the Levitical high priest. My grandmother, who was sitting beside me, could tell that I was bored. Halfway through the meeting, she opened her purse and handed me a tract to read. Having nothing else to occupy myself with, I took it.

I skimmed it over quickly. I can't remember what it was about, only that it ended with John 5:24: "Verily, verily I say unto you, he that heareth my word, and believeth on him that sent me, shall have everlasting life, and shall not come into condemnation but is passed from death unto life."

I stopped to get hold of the words in my mind, but they slid from my grip. I'd encountered the verse before, even committed it to memory. But now I realized I hadn't a clue what it meant. I read it again, more slowly this time, just trying to focus on its surface meaning. I read the verse a third time, a fourth, a fifth. It became a mantra. The words began to blur and lost all discursive content. Raw consonants and vowels rolled around in my head like bits of glass in a kaleidoscope, refracting shapes and colors without making a picture. Soon I had entered a euphoric state, past thought and feeling. My body was light, my heart a balloon, my mind wheeling and passive at the same moment.

Then it happened. The closest I can come to describing it is to say that it felt like trying to open a door that has a sticky lock. You put the key in the door and jangle it around for what seems like forever. It's not clear if the problem is with the key or the lock itself. Just when you're about to give up—the same moment—the key turns with sudden and total fluidity, as if there had never been an obstacle. That's what it was: a key turning in a lock.

After this happened, I slowly became conscious again of my body and surroundings. The words on the page came back into focus. I couldn't tell how long I'd been away. Moments perhaps. I felt a rush of emotion—not joy, exactly, or relief or hope or peace or anything else that I'd been told to expect. It was a kind of expansiveness. As if someone had knocked down a wall and added another room.

The next thing I remember is that I was crying and that people were looking at me. My grandmother gripped my arm and pursed her lips to suppress her joy, then narrowed her eyes and fixed me with a look that said she *knew*. With economy of motion, she picked up her purse, took out a pen and notepad, and handed them to me. She whispered into my ear, "Write down everything just like it happened."

I wish I knew what she was thinking. Maybe, by putting my experience into words, she thought it would gain an independent authority. The teenage heart needed a strong tether to reality. After getting saved, a believer could expect to be cross-examined by elders in the assembly. They would do their best to throw you off guard, to catch you up in a minor slip. If you wavered in your testimony, they'd raise an eyebrow and express concern that, in their judgment, your profession might not be solid enough to rest on.

To endure the gauntlet, you needed a good story. A solid testimony had three parts: "A time *when*, a place *where*, and a manner *how*." And so I wrote:

> At 8:34 pm on Tuesday, April 9, 1985 Brett Grainger was saved by the grace of God: "Verily, verily I say unto you, he that heareth my word, & believeth on him that sent me, shall have everlasting life and shall not come into condemnation but is passed from death unto life." John 5:24

It wasn't much of a story, to be sure: just the facts. Dry as a legal contract. Behold, the vehicle of grace by which the eternal Word penetrated my heart. The verse you chose was important—certain general conditions had to be met. A verse that had words such as *believe* or *accept* or *life* was a safe bet. I knew I was reasonably safe on that score. Lots of people got saved reading John 5:24. Having taken care to document the time *when* and the manner *how*, I can't be sure why I neglected to note the *where* of my regeneration. Perhaps it seemed obvious. Several dozen saints had had front-row seats. What defendant could ask for better witnesses?

Still, the language was so matter-of-fact, so precise: "8:34" rather than "Tuesday night" or even "8:30." It gave the note the air of a police report or a death certificate: In such and such room on such and such night, this particular boy died to the flesh, sloughed off Adam's debt, and was reborn whole and sinless and perfect.

The writing begins faintly, as if the dry stylus had resisted my effort to record the mystery. Halfway through, the letters switch from block capitals into the exaggerated loops of adolescent handwriting. The note has generous margins, creating the impression of ease and comfort. As you reach the last line, the writing suddenly constricts; *condemnation* curls up the right side in a playful parabola. I initially misspelled my last name, leaving out the *i*. The inserted vowel looks crowded. An afterthought.

I returned the pen to my grandmother, and she held my hand until the meeting ended. I felt pressured to share my good news, so I went up to as many people as I could, saying, "I got saved tonight," over and over. My grandmother stood at my side, showing me off as if I were a prize pumpkin at a fair. Everyone offered congratulations. My conversion had taken them by surprise. It was Tuesday night. People normally got saved on Sunday after the gospel meeting. But the Lord worked in mysterious ways.

I had a pretty good idea of what was expected of me. Soon, I would step forward and ask the elders for baptism. If they approved my request, the next stage was to request admission into fellowship, which meant I could break bread on Sunday morning with the other believers. I was expected to tell my friends how I'd gotten saved, and try to lead them to the Lord. Eventually, I would take the podium on Sunday night and preach the gospel. A first-time preacher usually told the story of his testimony. As I gained confidence, I would take more meetings and weigh in with my thoughts during the Bible reading.

Except I didn't do any of that. The truth was I didn't feel like a new creature. I saw the world through the same eyes, chafed against the same passions. It had been different for my grandmother. For one thing, she had come from an unbelieving home: her conversion had been the mature fruit of a spiritual quest, a search for authenticity. It was natural that she would want her family to know the same joy of self-discovery. But religious experience is a tailored garment. Paul's vivid tale of saving grace was a true fit for her ample and unambiguous faith, and she cut a pleasing figure in it. On me, the pattern hung loose, like a secondhand suit.

Chapter 4

THE PURSUIT OF PURITY

M Y FIRST ENCOUNTER with lust was Anna Kovacevic. Her angular features and giraffelike stature gave her the kind of exotic beauty often mistaken for ugliness in a small town. Because she did not have large breasts or wear tight-fitting jeans, Anna was invisible to the other boys in my class.

I had been interested in girls since the second grade, when I kissed Trudy Jackson under the teacher's desk while Mrs. Cassidy was in the bathroom. But this was different. When Anna came around, I was compelled to do strange things, such as try to smell her. This happened more often than I care to admit. Since her desk sat directly behind my own, I would regularly turn around to borrow things I didn't need, things I suspected she might have to retrieve by bending down to reach her backpack on the floor. I felt not in my right mind.

Brethren teaching on sex was elliptical. Admonitions were delivered in code. A preacher who railed against wearing makeup and jewelry was really talking about sex. The same went for dancing. I memorized verses that condemned fornicators long before I understood what it meant to fornicate. Did it include masturbation? I wondered.

The only time anyone made explicit reference to sex was when a brother or sister was being "read out" of the assembly, the Brethren ritual of excommunication. Theoretically, a person could be read out for any number of reasons, but the only cases I ever heard about involved adultery. On a Sunday morning, after the breaking of bread, the children and visitors were asked to leave the room, and an elder read out the sins of the accused. If there was no dissent from the assembly (and sometimes even if there was), the offender was declared to be out of fellowship and "under discipline."

Believers under discipline were shunned. In some cases, it was forbidden even to shake their hand. The excommunicated couldn't break bread or attend social functions such as fellowship teas or Bible conferences. They were, however, expected to attend all the regular meetings, sitting at the back of the hall in a show of penance. Depending on local custom and the severity of the offense, excommunication could last anywhere from two weeks to several months. After that, if all went well, a believer could expect to be "read back in" by the elders and return to normal life.

The Brethren obsession with adultery was in some ways perplexing, given that the Bible seemed to go so easy on it. When Joshua conquered Jericho, the only inhabitants spared were the harlot Rahab and her family. In the Gospels, Jesus hung out with at least one former prostitute and stopped an angry mob from stoning another woman caught in adultery. Even King David got off easy. After he slept with Bathsheba and had her husband murdered to hush things up, God got pretty upset, but in the end, he let David off scot-free.

The same could not be said of poor Onan. God might forgive craven adulterers such as David, but he showed no mercy on masturbators. When Onan spilled his seed on the ground, God struck him dead. It was a disturbing precedent—not that I feared a similar fate. But it undoubtedly diminished the pleasures of self-abuse.

As I often did in such moments, I turned to the Holy Scriptures for guidance. This is not exactly as it sounds. I had fallen into the habit of bibliomancy, the attempt to answer a question by picking a passage at random from the Bible. No one ever taught me to do this. It came quite naturally. For starters, the Scriptures were the literal Word of God. And I had always been encouraged to take my problems to the Bible. The Brethren affirmed that no knot was tighter than its sagely advice could untangle, no wound deeper than its medicine could penetrate.

In ancient times, bibliomancy was common practice. The Greeks did it with the writings of Homer, as did the Romans with Virgil and the Hindus with the Vedas. The conversion of St. Augustine turned on a game of biblical roulette. While resting in a Milanese garden, he heard a child's voice say, "Pick it up, read it; pick it up, read it." Augustine wrote, "I snatched it up, opened it, and in silence read the paragraph on which my eyes first fell: 'Not in rioting and drunkenness, not in chambering and wantonness, not in strife and envying, but put on the Lord Jesus Christ, and make no provision for the flesh to fulfill the lusts thereof.' "[1] Who could argue with that?

Later Christians elaborated upon the ritual, sometimes using a golden pin to find the hidden verse in the haystack. Bibliomancy was enough of a problem in seventeenth-century New England for the Puritan divine Increase Mather to include it on a list of prohibited practices. For certain, no self-respecting fundamentalist countenanced such brazen superstition. Yet it persisted among those who searched the Scriptures for a good word.

The ritual I followed was perhaps the simplest. I would close my eyes and form a question in my mind, then take the book and open it at random. Running my hand across a page, I would open my eyes as soon as the index finger came to rest.

Often the oracles spoke subtly. One of my first attempts turned up Ezra 8:11: "And the sons of Bebai; Zecharaiah the son of Bebai, and with him twenty and eight males." What could God be trying to tell me? Such disappointments I usually put down to a test run. After half a dozen attempts, I would land on something relevant to my predicament.

But when I approached the Bible for direction in the delicate business of self-mastery, lightning struck the very first time. After going through the motions, my eyes lighted immediately upon Job 38:3: "Gird up now your loins like a man; for I will demand of thee, and answer thou me."

I could hard by believe it. The thing had worked. I felt like Moses on Mount Sinai, the stone tablets still smoking in my hands. I laid down the Bible with a sudden surge of resolve, a girding of the will. In that moment, I knew I had become master of my domain, a perception that endured for several weeks until Onan made a quiet return.

As much as every believer loved John 3:16, the plain truth was that the Brethren belonged more to Paul than to the Gospels. If the Brethren had a manifesto, it came from the sixth chapter of Paul's Second Letter to the Corinthians: "Wherefore come out from among them and be ye separate, saith the Lord, and touch not the unclean thing; and I will receive you." If believers hoped to be received by God, they had to turn their backs to the world. They put away the ordinary to become extraordinary. "Be ye perfect," Jesus said, "as your father in heaven is perfect."

The Brethren hinted at this vision of moral and spiritual perfection when they referred to themselves as "the saints," a bold, if logical, extension of Martin Luther's doctrine of a "priesthood of all believers." Any man or woman who professed a saving knowledge of Jesus Christ was not just a priest but also a saint. The New Covenant guaranteed every Christian eternal life, liberty, and the pursuit of purity.

In its simplest form, purity was a condition of separation from sin. It was a singular concept, like truth. Imagine two sticks, one straight and one crooked. A crooked stick could be crooked in a thousand different ways, but a stick could only be straight in one way. Goodness was simple, evil exceedingly complex. It took a multitude of forms. Before Jesus healed the possessed man, he asked the demon its name. "We are legion," the demon replied.

Because of the complex forms of wickedness in the world, the Brethren took precautions. They met in a simple hall whose plainness was the careful outworking of a theology of separation from the world. There was none of the architectural shorthand that marked other houses of worship, no cross or steeple. The interior preached a similar iconoclasm. No stained glass, no organ or piano to accompany the hymns. Only a few framed verses of Scripture adorned the walls. Such deprivations expressed the Brethren belief that they had been called out, set apart.

Even the location of our assembly expressed a desire for higher ground, a restless clamoring to climb our way out of the world. Like a palisade lookout in the middle of Indian country, the Gospel Hall occupied the summit of a small hill in the center of town. Around lay a wilderness of vice and declension. On Main Street, kids cruised in hot rods or queued in front of the movie theater. Just over the crest of the hill lay the Bayview Hotel, a place that projected so much ritual impurity it spilled out onto the sidewalk.

Even inside the hall, the Brethren were not safe from pollution. During the "breaking of bread," the weekly Communion service held on Sunday morning, saved and unsaved were separated like wheat and chaff. I took my place with my father at the back of the hall, while my mother sat up in the small square of chairs reserved for those who had made a profession of faith, undergone baptism, and been accepted into fellowship. After an hour and a half of silence, punctuated by occasional hymns and extemporaneous prayers, an elderly brother stood and prayed for the loaf of white bread that sat on the white, linen-covered table in the middle of the room. He took the loaf in his hands and broke it in two, handing a piece to a believer on either side of him, who plucked a morsel from the soft middle and passed the rest along. If there were brothers or sisters visiting from another assembly, they were expected to produce a letter of commendation in order to break bread.

Such vigilance in fencing the table was rare among Protestants, who generally took the view that the bread and wine are not the literal body and blood of God, but mere symbols, a memorial supper. But symbols were what the Brethren cared most about. In the world, it was hard to tell the difference between a believer and an unbeliever. They weren't Mennonites, who wore strange clothes and lived in isolated communities. The wheat and the tares grew together. Saved and unsaved sat beside one another in school, toiled on the same assembly line, drank the same soda. Because daily life made it impossible to distinguish the elect, the small markers of identity—what Freud called "the narcissism of minor difference"—acquired tremendous significance. Such markers were often negative; it wasn't what you *did* but what you *didn't* do— drinking, dancing, smoking, or swearing, no sex outside of marriage, no revealing clothing or makeup for women. These small acts of renunciation allowed believers to be in the world but not of it.

Reading the signs of election could be challenging. Though we knew we were not of the world, the borders of worldliness could be mysterious and ill defined, like the shadows objects cast on a cloudy day. Good and evil were absolute, but worldliness was a moving target. Sometimes you could almost see the line being redrawn in the sand. In my mother's day, only unbelievers had televisions. By the time I came along, the majority of saints—apart from a few old-school preachers such as my grandfather—had a heavy, wood-paneled set in the living room, just like their neighbors. Worldliness migrated to the big screen. At recess, I played Star Wars without ever having seen Han Solo or the *Millennium Falcon*.

This never really bothered me until the day that my best friend asked me to see *Clash of the Titans* at the drive-in. I was nine, and though I knew it was out of the question I begged my mother to let me go. I knew she felt town about it. On the one hand, she had no particular objections, no fear that I would be morally compromised by on innocent outing to the cinema. Yet, she knew that if someone in the assembly found out that I had been to the movies, the family would be humiliated.

A few years later, VCRs came on the market. Given the number of Brethren who already had televisions, the local elders took no clear position on the morality of the new devices. This meant I could finally watch *Titans*. In the living room, safe from any fear of ritual pollution, I watched the pagan Perseus decapitate Medusa and use her writhing head to turn the Kraken to stone.

Some of the older prohibitions were bizarre even to believers. In the 1960s, some assemblies forbade the wearing of red on the Sabbath. Facial hair also pricked their suspicions. In the 1980s, my Sunday school teacher got into trouble with an elder for his unkempt beard. The elder quoted 1 Corinthians 11: "Does not even nature itself teach you that if a man has long hair, it is a disgrace to him?" My teacher brushed the blow aside and returned a one-two jab of Leviticus 19, where God forbids the Israelites from trimming the corners of their beards, and 2 Samuel 10, in which King David is humiliated when his servants are captured by his enemies and given a full shave.

A third brother helpfully pointed out that the elder himself had facial hair. It wasn't much: a thin line of stubble shading his upper lip. But if God disapproved of beards, the brother reasoned, he wasn't likely to appreciate mustaches, either. The next Sunday morning, both men turned up bashful and clean-shaven, like newly sheared sheep.

The Brethren stood in a long line of "come-outers." Most notable, perhaps, were the religious dissenters who in the later sixteenth century broke with the Church of England, believing it to be beyond reformation. These Puritan separatists, who sailed to America in the *Mayflower* and established the first permanent

English-speaking settlement at Plymouth, Massachusetts, were religious ascetics. They envisioned life as an endless task of polishing the body and mind like a mirror until they reflected the light of heaven.

The Puritans employed a wide palette of behavior to express their ideas about purity. Food was particularly important. Ministers preached against the sin of gluttony, while congregants used fasting as an all-purpose tool to address a range of religious needs. They fasted to heal divisions within a church, or to stave off drought or sickness (both were seen as signs of God's disfavor); they fasted to mark a change in seasons, to protect ships at sea, or in aid of soldiers sent off to fight the Indians. Fast days helped preserve a godly people and mark off the church from the world. When church members were put under discipline but refused to confess, the entire congregation might fast to encourage a confession. American presidents proclaimed national days of prayer and fasting. In 1863, in the midst of the Civil War, Abraham Lincoln called for a fast day to "seek pardon for our national sins" and asked Americans to "abstain, on that day, from their ordinary secular pursuits, and to unite, at their several places of public worship and their respective homes, in keeping the day holy to the Lord."

Puritans were not teetotalers. Compared to fundamentalists, their attitudes about alcohol were permissive, to say the least. Though drunkenness was condemned, alcohol was universally consumed and admired. In a sermon from 1673, Increase Mather went so far as to call it "a good creature of God." In matters of food and drink, purity meant balance and thoughtful moderation, the avoidance of extremes. In the nineteenth century, American attitudes about eating and drinking went through a profound transformation. Fasting, in general, declined, in part a result of

84

Protestant resentment of the growing presence of Catholics (for whom fasting was an important religious practice) and the spread of secularization, which viewed fasting as irrational superstition, a holdover from a premodern era. Religious ascetics made way for the gurus of the fitness movement, who preached dieting as a secular substitute for the fast.

As food became disenchanted, the burden of communicating Protestant notions of purity shifted increasingly to alcohol. In the second half of the nineteenth century, the temperance and prohibition movements closed down bars and taverns that throve under the Puritans. Evangelicals helped develop and popularize a new scientific view of alcohol as addictive and toxic. Even the most ancient Christian practices were affected. In 1869, for the first time in history, grape juice was substituted for wine in the Lord's Supper (a task for which Welch's grape juice was expressly invented). The old ethic of moderation was out; abstinence was in.

As believers accepted the new secular attitudes about food, they not only lost an important tool to mark off the sacred from the profane; they became more gluttonous. According to a study by Purdue University, fundamentalists are the fattest religious people in America. In 1986, the obesity rate among Baptists was 24 percent; by 1994, it had risen to 30 percent, the same as the national average. By comparison, Catholic rates of obesity during the same period held steady at 17 percent; Jewish obesity remained at 1 percent, and rates among other non-Christian religious groups rose but remained below 1 percent.[2] When it comes to overeating, fundamentalists are far more worldly than their non-Christian neighbors.

By embracing so many of the assumptions and habits of secular American culture, fundamentalists have opened themselves up to fears of cultural assimilation. To strengthen their flagging sense of collective identity, believers pick points of minor difference and turn them into major public battles whose spoils are often symbolic—the right to pray at a football game, for example, or to erect a public monument to the Ten Commandments. Like a city that has shut down its expressways, fundamentalists have cut themselves off from many of the avenues that Protestants have traditionally used to distance themselves from the world. When rush hour hits, the few paths to purity that remain open are quickly jammed with traffic.

Fundamentalists are suburban ascetics. Rather than retreat from the world, they make their way in the air-conditioned wilderness of the mall and beauty parlor. Like the spiritual athletes who preceded them, they do daily battle with the demons of sexual desire and "unwanted same-sex attraction." John the Baptist, the first great Christian ascetic, wore his hair shirt the traditional way, next to his skin. Suburban ascetics turn their hair shirt inside out and show it to the world. The young disciples of the modern abstinence movement wear T-shirts with slogans like BORN-AGAIN VIRGIN and PET YOUR DOG, NOT YOUR DATE. They keep a silver ring on the third finger of their left hand, inscribed with the words of 1 Thessalonians 4:3–4 ("God wants you to be holy, so you should keep clear of all sexual sin. Then each of you will control your body and live in holiness and honor") to signify their marriage to Jesus Christ. They sign virginity pledges at rock concerts hosted by groups like True Love Waits. At "purity balls," teenage girls dress up in gowns and tiaras and pledge their celibacy to their fathers, who, in turn, vow to "be pure in my own life as a man, husband,

and father" and to be their daughters' "authority and protection in the area of purity." Then they dance and eat wedding cake.

Fundamentalism's poverty of symbols to express purity goes some of the way to explaining why believers seem to have such a one-track mind about sex. Sexual morality is at the core of fundamentalist culture and identity, establishing clear boundaries between insiders and outsiders, sacred and profane, clean and unclean, good and evil. Of the dominant political issues concerning fundamentalists today, three of them—abortion, pornography, and gay marriage—focus either on sex or its immediate effects.

Sex can also overtake fundamentalist activities where the purported focus is something other than sex. Take the case of Hell House. Ostensibly, the aim is evangelism, turning sinners to Christ. But the morality play also targets believers. In the production I visited, most of the story lines focused on the dangers of sex. In the opening scene, set in a high school, a teenage girl in a miniskirt flirted with a male student in front of his locker. A swaggering jock arrived and accused the boy of moving in on his girlfriend. The scene ended with the jock beating up the student. The moral wasn't clear until our guide explained that the girl had been sexually abused by her father: incest leads to sexual promiscuity and youth violence.

In another room, a man drank from a bottle of Jack Daniel's while surfing for porn on his computer. Just then, his teenage daughter came in. The father, drunk and aroused, tried to have sex with her. The girl's boyfriend showed up with a gun, which the father pried away, shooting both of them to death with it. In case anyone missed the point (pornography leads to incest and homicide), the story continued in the next room, a domestic scene in which two teenage girls were discussing online dating.

One of them had arranged a blind date that evening with a mystery man, who turned out to be none other than the porn-addled, alcoholic murderer from the previous scene. The girl rebuffed his advances, remarking that he looked much older than his on-screen photo, a comment that provoked the man to strangle her to death.

The morality play reached its apogee on a stage modeled after a medical clinic. Yet another teenage heroine lay on her back in a hospital gown, her feet in stirrups. A doctor reached between her legs and produced clumps of bloody tissue. Overhead, television screens projected images of aborted fetuses. A boyfriend character, standing by in support, became disgusted and fled the room. The girl, now screaming and hysterical, twisted briefly in her stirrups and died abruptly, either from an internal hemorrhage or a broken heart.

Hell House is a topsy-turvy take on mainstream attitudes about sex, a fundie fun house that hawks titillation and terror as effectively as any bottom-rack horror flick. Girls play sexualized victims; boys are predators or patsies. Defenders see such methods as a necessary counterweight to the celebration of teenage sexuality in American popular culture, the films, music, and television shows that make sex the Holy Grail of high school experience. But by leading children down the opposite path—teaching them that sex is the ultimate sacrilege committed against a person's body, family, and God—the theater of abstinence effects a similar result: an unhealthy obsession with sex.

When I was three years old, my mother was read out of the Brethren. The trouble started when the elders invited a preacher named Archie Godfrey to host a series of special meetings, as they were called. The only thing special about special meetings was that they went on night after night, often for weeks or months on end. Like everything the Brethren did, they were a sober business, a revival without the *Hallelujahs* or *Lord have mercys*.

A visiting preacher was treated like a movie star. The men invited him to weigh in on their theological disputes; the women vied to host him in their homes, where they starched his shirts, fluffed his pillows, and cooked his favorite meals. This special treatment was justified because the preacher had the most important job on earth, a job so important that believers spoke of it simply as "the work." He was their evangelist, sent to herd up God's lost sheep, and once he got going, there was no telling when he might finish. A preacher expected to continue the work until a respectable number had been saved or the elders asked him to leave, whichever came first.

Archie Godfrey was short and aging, with a high-pitched voice and a gaunt complexion that cracked into a million wrinkles when he smiled. Like other preachers, he started slow and built up speed gradually like a freight train, until veins bulged from his forehead and his face flushed like a thumb hit by a hammer. Just as he seemed primed for cardiac arrest, Archie would thrust out his arms like a bird and vanish behind the pulpit. For half a minute or more, the stage would be empty save for his shrill, disembodied yowl and his lily-white hands, which flapped madly on either side of the pulpit like a pair of severed wings.

Despite rarely getting to see their families, most Brethren preachers were married. Archie had always been a notable exception. However, shortly after he arrived in town, word spread that the old bachelor had fallen for a middle-aged widow he'd recently met in another assembly. As soon as his work was finished, the couple planned to wed.

The meetings got off to a rough start. Efforts to attract the unsaved had been largely unsuccessful, and the weeks rolled on without a single new profession of faith. Archie began to feel the heat. He focused on any new faces in the crowd and preached to them directly, a practice that usually guaranteed they wouldn't be back the next night. The sweat poured out of him. The veins in his forehead and arms strained like ropes against his Herculean exertions. The disappearing-bird trick became more protracted, until it seemed he might vanish from the stage completely. No matter what he tried, no one was getting religion.

Archie was in a bind. He needed an exit strategy. It was already a month, and he had a fiancée waiting at the altar. Yet he couldn't bring the meetings to an end without something to show the elders, a few loose souls in his pocket. The elders also felt the pressure. Concluding the meetings without at least one new profession of faith was an admission of poor judgment: they had failed to discern that the time was not ripe for the work of the Spirit.

As the work entered its fifth week, Archie tried something different. He turned on the saints. Perhaps the Holy Spirit had not seen fit to bless these meetings for a reason, he suggested. Perhaps a young person in the meeting had made a false profession of faith? Or perhaps sin had entered the camp? If there was impurity in the assembly, he warned, the Lord would withhold his Spirit and no new souls would be brought to Christ.

The saints stiffened in their chairs. Sidelong glances were exchanged as people wondered who the culprit might be. Many searched their own hearts. My mother, who'd been at the meetings

almost every night, formed a thought in her mind: What if it was
her fault? What if she harbored an unconfessed sin? She rifled
through the drawers of memory, searching for the dirty sock. Finally, it came to her. It was years ago, in her teens. She had been
dating my father, and their relationship had become physical. The
sweetness of youthful indiscretion soured as she now realized the
bitter fruit it had born. Not only had she damaged her own testimony, she was keeping others from Jesus. She was to blame.

Fortunately, she thought, the timing was good. Her parents were
on vacation in Florida. That would spare them the initial embarrassment. My father was also away. In the summer he rode with a
crew on a striper, the customized rig used to paint the lines on as-
phalt roads, which took him for days at a time. One night, after
putting my brother and me to bed, she called Archie and told him
her secret. He listened attentively. "You know what this means?"
he said.

She did. Archie took her confession to the elders, who thanked
him and then deliberated in private. The following Sunday morning, my mother was read out of the assembly. She sat in the back
while an elder detailed her transgressions. She felt as if someone
had sewn a letter on her chest. A few days later in the drugstore,
she crossed paths with a woman from the meeting. They'd known
each other since childhood. Their eyes met briefly. Then the
woman turned and walked off without saying a word.

The special meetings carried on for another week. Archie
seemed relaxed, even ebullient, despite having led no new souls
to the Lord. The elders were also content. When Archie asked
for permission to conclude the meetings, they smiled graciously
and thanked him for a job well done.

Archie returned home to his fiancée, who was busy finalizing the details for the wedding scheduled for the following weekend. That night she told Archie that there was something about her that he needed to know. Years back, while her husband was still alive, she'd had a brief affair with another man in the assembly. She had never confessed her adultery to anyone.

The shock put Archie in the hospital. When he got out a few days later, he went to the local elders, and in short order the fiancée was read out. However, in deference to the impending nuptials and to Archie's delicate condition, her sentence was abbreviated, and after only a week, she was restored to fellowship. My mother waited a full month before she could return to the holy huddle and break bread with the saints.

Chapter 5

FREELANCE FUNDAMENTALISM

I N 1997, the Canadian province of Ontario upgraded its driver's license. The old-fashioned laminated card with its head-and-shoulders Polaroid was discarded in favor of one that employed new digital imaging technology. As well as eliminating the cost of film, the province's Ministry of Transportation hoped that recent advances in digital photography would allow them to build an easily accessible database of driver portraits. Most Ontarians greeted the policy with a polite shrug.

That year, George Bothwell went into a local government building in Owen Sound, a small port city on the bleak, granite shores of Lake Huron, to get his license renewed. George was a fifty-year-old organic farmer with a handsome weathered face and a short white beard that gave him a resemblance to Ernest Hemingway. He noticed the new camera as soon as he entered the licensing office. It was mounted in a large steel box emblazoned with the name of its manufacturer, Imaging Automation. A thick black cable emerged from the back of the box and snaked out of the room. George asked the woman behind the desk where the cable went. The woman said she didn't know, but she thought it relayed the digital images to a central ministry database.

George heard warning bells. He walked out of the office without his license renewal and drove home to the farm. Then he went online and visited the Web site for Imaging Automation. The company trumpeted the business advantages promised by its technologies: "Photographic images will be transferred over networks and wireless to wherever they are needed, to verify checks being cashed, licenses renewed, and hundreds of other applications."

The "hundreds of other applications" concerned George. He didn't like the idea of a third party having access to his image. He wrote a letter to Imaging Automation requesting more information, and the company sent him some brochures. One of them referred to a device called an Argus Platform.

"Well, I asked them if it had any relation to Argus of Greek mythology," George said. "You know, the guy with a hundred eyes that always slept with two closed, so as to keep constant watch with the other ninety-eight."

Then George did what he often does when his suspicions are aroused. He took out his Bible. On this particular day, he was interested in the thirteenth chapter of the book of Revelation, perhaps the most discussed prophetic chapter in the New Testament. It offers a harrowing description of a mysterious figure known as the beast, who will use his charisma and supernatural abilities to create a vast political empire that modern readers might describe using the adjective *Orwellian*:

And he causeth all, both small and great, rich and poor, free and bond, to receive a mark in their right hand, or in their foreheads: And that no man might buy or sell, save he that had the mark, or the name of the beast, or the number of his name. Here is wisdom.

George fetched his Bible concordance and looked up the meaning of the Greek word for *mark*. The first definition indicated "an etching or a stamp, as a badge of servitude." He read further: "an exact copy or representation; an express image." He thought about Imaging Automation, how the company claimed to be able to transmit a perfect digital replication of a person's image around the world in the blink of an eye.

"I'll tell you, I got goose bumps," he said, holding out a bare forearm. "We're moving to a one-world government under the rule of Lucifer—the Bible tells us. And he's going to establish a system where you're not going to buy or sell except under his authority. And that authority is going to come through the use of a mark from your right hand and your forehead and his number. That to me is fairly clear."

George contacted the Ministry of Transportation to request an exemption from the photo requirement on religious grounds. The ministry had a special application form for such requests. After several months, George got a letter back saying that his application had been rejected. He made a number of appeals, which were also rejected on the grounds that he required the backing of a recognized church or religious leader.

"I went around for six months like an idiot, trying to get a leader," George said. "Baptists, Mennonites, you name it. Couldn't find a leader." After six years of this kind of wrangling, George held a press conference with his lawyer to announce that he was taking the government to court for violating his religious freedom. He wore a tweed jacket and jeans tucked into black cowboy boots and carried a Bible bound in worn red leather. While his lawyer made a presentation, George stared at the floor, occasionally raising a hand to shield his face from the reporters' cameras. When the lawyer finished, George answered questions.

What did he have against digital photography? "This technology will allow central control over people's behavior, which the Bible warns us against." Why did he think that digital images were the work of Satan?" George replied that the use of biometrics—the technique of identifying people based on the geometry of the face, hand, or retina—was the "mark of the beast," a sign of spiritual slavery to the Antichrist. Those who allowed their distinctive biometric marks to be stored in a central government database, he said, would "drink the wine of the wrath of God."

"Mr. Bothwell, how did you feel coming before this press conference today, knowing that there would be digital cameras here?"

The irony wasn't lost on George. He conceded his discomfort with the situation, but after politely asking for an exemption from the photo requirement for six years, he was prepared to take a few chances.

"Is it true that you don't belong to any recognized church?"

The lawyer stepped in before George could answer. It shouldn't matter, he said, how his client chose to worship God. Personal faith was not a popularity contest. "It is no business of the government to judge the truth of a religious belief by requiring more than one person to hold it." The lawyer paused, adopting a more solicitous tone. "George doesn't have a congregation. He doesn't have a religious leader other than Jesus

Christ—who, as he points out, is not about to write a letter of support for him to the Ontario government."

George smiled. He knew how ridiculous all this looked to an outsider. He once thought as they did, before he realized that all the coincidences in his life—the endless run-ins with the government and the banks—were not in fact coincidences but part of a larger plan to denude men and women of their God-given rights and freedoms and to submit them to the one-world rule of the Antichrist. Someone asked the lawyer if he was worried about his client's credibility in court. "I don't think anyone will dismiss him as a wingnut," the lawyer said. "These views are widely held."

George hadn't always been a fundamentalist. He was raised in the most liberal church in the country, the United Church of Canada. He left in 1980 over objections with his minister, who, as he puts it, was soft on communism and rarely preached from the Bible. George then attached himself to a Baptist congregation, a relationship that ended in the late 1990s, after the minister refused to endorse George's application for a photo-license exemption. George had laid out all his evidence linking biometrics with the mark of the beast. He'd even given the congregation a presentation on how to locate 666—the "number of the beast"—in any Universal Product Code. But the minister assured him that born-again Christians didn't have to worry about such things. The Rapture, he said, would take place long before the Antichrist showed up.

George doesn't like the Rapture—not just because he thinks it's unbiblical, but because he thinks it's downright cowardly. The Rapture says that the church won't be around to resist evil in the world when evil most needs to be resisted. To George's mind, a Christian shouldn't be afraid of a good fight. He relishes being an underdog, a lonely David against the Goliaths of the world. For this and other reasons, he believes that the vast majority of Christian churches have fallen into spiritual ruin. They are far too interested in social respectability. "They are apostate," he said. "They worship mammon instead of God."

By refusing to identify himself with a minister or a congregation, George seems to be on the wrong side of two millennia of church tradition. But looked at another way, he fits the model of a certain Christian archetype, the early ascetics who retreated into the desert as a protest against the corruption of the world, or the Protestant martyrs who took a stand against the excesses of the Catholic Church. George's manifesto is an outworking of the one that Martin Luther used to launch the Reformation: that God can directly be experienced and apprehended by reading the Bible. No intermediary—pastor, priest, or bishop—is required. In his own way, George is simply carrying the Protestant principle of *sola scriptura*, "by scripture alone," to its logical conclusion. He has become a church of one.

George became a fundamentalist in the early 1980s, when the world as he knew it was ending. The first crisis was personal. On a pretty June day in 1980, George was outside chopping silage. His three-year-old daughter, Megan, woke up with a high temperature and feeling sick to her stomach. George called the pediatrician, who discouraged him from taking Megan to the hospital. But the fever got worse, and so the following morning, after a sleepless night, George took his daughter to the ER. Initially the doctors were unconcerned, but by evening they had diagnosed her with spinal meningitis. The hospital tried to arrange an air-lift to a larger hospital but couldn't locate a helicopter. The paramedics finally packed Megan in an ambulance and set off, with George and his wife, Azelda, tailing close behind. It was too late.

An inquest was held into Megan's death, which absolved the hospital of any wrongdoing. George, however, continued to be-lieve that the doctors had failed her: "My cows got better medical attention than they gave my daughter." Aggrieved and distressed, he turned to his Bible and found comfort in the dark passages that prophesy a time of creeping disorder, corruption, and injustice, when men will turn away from God. "My daugh-ter died. It's a pretty hard thing to rationalize," he said. "I was looking around, and the Bible really seemed to answer a whole lot of questions that nobody else wanted to answer—even the ministers."

While dealing with his loss, Bothwell faced a second disaster: the farm-debt crisis of the early 1980s. During the previous de-cade, governments and banks in North America had pushed to modernize agriculture, moving away from the traditional model of small family farms growing a diversity of crops to sprawling megafarms specializing in monocrops. Owing to their enormous size and reliance on new technology, the megafarms carried mas-sive debts. So long as interest rates remained low, as they did for much of the 1970s, farmers could make their payments and still turn a healthy profit.

In 1980, the economy crashed and interest rates went through the roof. The megafarms went down like dominoes. Entire communities were bankrupted overnight. Many farmers committed suicide. The crisis radicalized George. He became a founding member of the Canadian Farm Survival Association, which led a public campaign to raise awareness and lobby the government to intervene. In truth, however, George had already lost faith in the ability of elected government to act for the common good. Reading his Bible, he learned how during the End Times, men would abandon righteousness and worship mammon. Only a few prophetic voices, a faithful remnant, would stand in the gap and speak truth to power. One day at lunch hour, George drove his beat-up tractor through the shadowed valley of skyscrapers in Toronto's central banking district. He brought traffic to a standstill as drivers and pedestrians craned their necks to read the handmade signs he'd fastened to every surface of the machine—ABOLISH USURY: JAIL LOAN-SHARK BANKERS, NEW WORLD ORDER: IMF AND UNITED NATIONS ÜBER ALLES, and MERCHANTS OF BABYLON: BORN OF THEIR FATHER THE DEVIL.

Unlike his neighbors, George could still afford to pay the loans on his farm. However, on principle, he decided he would stop paying the exorbitant rates of interest. His bank tried to repossess his tractor. Then, to make an example of him, it had him arrested for bank fraud, claiming that he had relocated a herd of cattle that had been used as collateral to another property without informing the bank. When George refused to give the police his fingerprints, he spent ninety days in solitary confinement, a period he describes as "one of the lowest points in my life." George refused to plea-bargain and went through twelve different defense lawyers before he managed to get all the charges against him dismissed.

Like Paul's multiple stints in Roman prisons or Martin Luther

King's incarceration in Birmingham, George saw his time in captivity as the seal of his calling as a prophet. He spent his time in solitary deepening his knowledge of the Scriptures, teasing out his intuitions and premonitions into a systematic theology. While idiosyncratic, his system followed the shape of other fundamentalist visions of the End Times: the world spiraling into darkness; wars and rumors of wars filling the land; social morality in decline; open apostasy in the churches; and all things groaning toward the birth of the Antichrist, whose bloody reign will end with the glorious appearance of Jesus Christ.

Fundamentalists are thought to read from a rigid script, but a striking feature of George's freelance faith is its unpredictability. On a number of political issues, George detours from typical conservative positions and invents his own. An example is his fervent criticism of capitalism, and of the banking industry in particular, which he says promotes a false religion of materialism. Another is his embrace of the organic-farming movement. George owns 600 acres and rents another 450, growing a mix of organic grain and soybeans. He switched to organics in 1985, when he became convinced that the chemicals and pesticides used in agribusiness were contrary to the laws of God and nature. "These guys are into doing stuff that curls my hair," he told me. "Genetic modification, polluting, feeding cattle with dead cattle—all for what? At the end of the year I make another ten bucks."

His crusade against the government has been costly. He estimates that his legal fees have mounted to more than $100,000. With proceeds from the farm being siphoned off, maintenance on the property has fallen behind. Out at the barn, the massive green doors sagged on their hinges. The farmhouse had also seen better days. The attic windows were blackened and boarded up, like empty eye sockets. "It's about priorities," George said. "There's lots of places I'd like to put the money. But let's do first things first."

Fundamentalists weren't the first modern Christians to show an interest in the book of Revelation. During the American Revolution, an anti-British pamphleteer saw its prophecies fulfilled in the hated Stamp Act. Patriots were warned not to accept documents bearing the king's stamp, "lest by touching any paper with this impression, you receive the mark of the beast." During the Great Depression, some of those who opposed FDR and the sweeping federal powers being assumed under the New Deal identified the mark with the logo of the National Recovery Administration.

But the real explosion of interest in the mark came during the Cold War. Bible-believing Christians read prophecy into their fears of godless communism and a creeping Orwellian police state. Secular and religious anxieties blended as the information revolution spawned a new culture of surveillance. Modern management theory, which centralized government and business in large, impersonal bureaucracies, was interpreted as a form of social control. Whenever government came up with a new way of tracking the free movement of citizens, from Social Security numbers to national identity cards, fundamentalists greeted the initiative as a possible candidate for the mark. Preachers warned that governments would soon begin tattooing or branding citizens with a UPC code or some kind of number, usually 666, or implanting an electronic device in their bodies, turning people into a "walking credit card." Computers became a source of acute concern, especially after the appearance of HAL, the homicidal artificial intelligence in Stanley Kubrick's film *2001: A Space Odyssey*. In 1981, another Hal, the fundamentalist Hal Lindsey, author of *The Late Great Planet Earth*, wrote, "The person who controls the main computer controls the world."

As new candidates for the mark continue to pop up like ducks in a shooting gallery, it would be tempting to dismiss these speculations as symptoms of a mass cultural hysteria, a Rorschach for every misunderstood aspect of modern life. But such explanations overlook how prophetic speculation fits into a broader spiritual discipline. In its original context, the mark was a cipher for idolatry; it represented those who bowed down and worshipped the Roman emperor or his image. When a fundamentalist asks his followers to be on the lookout for the mark of the beast, he is reminding them that their ultimate allegiance is not to any god of this world, but to an invisible kingdom.

A few years back, a truck pulled up at the end of George's driveway. A group of men climbed out with stakes and surveying equipment, setting up a new 911 emergency system. Local residents would be assigned a new street number to coordinate fire and ambulance service. George was suspicious, so he did some digging. At length, he found someone who told him that the 911 system employed a network of global-positioned satellites.

"They can make a digital map of any location in the world and put that image into the company's central global database," George said. "Which is in India."

George began to connect the dots between the 911 system and his ongoing entanglement with the Ministry of Transportation.

In each case, the privacy of the individual, namely himself, had been compromised. Just as the government wanted control over his facial image, the company behind the 911 system wanted control over precise geographical data relating to his farm. To those who said that private information would be encrypted and safeguarded, he replied that he had already been a victim of information-swapping between government departments. In the late 1990s, a few months after his driver's license lapsed, George was hit by an audit initiated by the government's Identification and Compliance Unit. In his mind, the two departments had clearly colluded.

After the audit, George began to ask himself where all this "identification and compliance" business was heading. What would happen when these omniscient databases came under the control of the Antichrist? Perhaps the beast would use his GPS satellites to track down the sort of folks who were making trouble for the authorities. People like him.

The next day, George went out into the yard and dug up the surveyor's stakes.

As George sees it, life offers precious few coincidences. His mind is like a spiderweb, catching anything that falls into it, binding up seemingly unrelated events from the daily news—the price of gold, the expansion of the European Union, the UN's failure to prevent the Rwandan genocide. The connection that George sees between biometrics and the farming crisis is the banking industry. It's all about mammon. "This biometrics thing is going to be the most lucrative thing in the history of the world," he said. "With Enron, those guys were only able to abscond with billions. This is trillions. They're going to manage every little individual and milk him to the boards."

There's no question that biometrics is big business. Industry revenues, worth less than $1 billion in 2003, were projected to break the $4 billion mark by 2007—a boom born of the present age of insecurity and the War on Terror. Beginning in 2004, the American government required all foreigners visiting the country on visas to have their faces and hands digitally scanned at the border. U.S. passports may soon include a computer chip carrying the user's biometric data. The American Civil Liberties Union (ACLU) has expressed concern over the growing culture of surveillance in America, a trend that could, it argues, undermine democratic freedoms and fuel identity theft. In 2004, the ACLU, along with twelve other organizations from North America, Europe, and Asia, signed a letter to the International Civil Aviation Organization saying they were "increasingly concerned that the biometric travel document initiative is part and parcel of a larger surveillance infrastructure monitoring the movement of individuals globally."

But George's concerns with biometrics go deeper. He is suspicious of government assurances that biometrics will bring in an age of peace and security. There will be no peace on earth, he says, until the Prince of Peace—Jesus Christ—brings it. "Keep in mind the Bible says, 'When they say peace and security, sudden destruction will come upon them.' We're being sold a bill of goods that won't be delivered."

Most Christians today would reject the suggestion that the Bible predicted the rise of retinal scanners. But George believes that John of Patmos, the writer of Revelation, anticipated developments such as this. "That prophecy was written two millennia ago, when there was really no vocabulary to describe the technology that has come up on this," he said. John had to encrypt his visions in a language that humans could easily decode twenty centuries later—writing generically of a "mark" on the "right hand" instead of fingerprints and facial scans. The only tool a person needs to break the code, George believes, is plain common sense.

Most fundamentalists defend their theories by arguing that they are simply reading the Bible. More often than not, however, they get a little help along the way. George's den is a small room crammed with boxes and piles of farm bills. The walls are lined with books written by popular fundamentalist writers such as Tim LaHaye and Ralph Epperson. One volume bears this authorial inscription: "For George & Azelda, Hope this will help you and loved ones in fighting the Antichrist." Fundamentalists argue that they don't do theology, which adds a layer of meaning to Scripture that does not exist in the literal text, but rather present its plain, unadorned surface meaning. But any reading requires interpretation, and prophetic books such as Revelation are dense and poetic and require extensive leaps of logic to translate into the currency of modern life.

George's fundamentalism offers him more than just a unique take on technology. It provides access to an entirely different version of modernity, a story characterized not by the expansion of progressive values such as human rights and democracy, but by a downward slide into dictatorship and social anarchy. The world can only get worse, not better. While others might despair at this dark momentum, George seems to take comfort from it; his faith allows him to see any disturbing development as part of God's irresistible plan to cleanse the world by submerging it in a flood of apocalyptic violence.

George has a keen sense of how others perceive him. One of his friends, a driver for a local fuel company, at the farm for a visit, offered his take on George's local reputation: "A lot of people think George is right off his rocker, because they think he can take things too far."

"That's right," George said. "I do take things too far."

"Most of us are ignorant of what's going on, because we live in such a busy society," the driver continued. "George is taking the time to investigate this stuff. He's just a little more aware of what's going on. You've got to have the boldness, and I think George has the boldness to stand up for some of this. I mean, how many people can go to court and spend the kind of money George has?"

"Most people don't want trouble in their lives," George said. "I don't either. But you got to draw the line someplace. Why don't I just roll over for the government on biometrics? Why didn't I roll over for the banks in the eighties when they were defrauding farmers with their high interest rates in order to centralize control of agriculture in this country? I would say there is right and wrong. They've been trying to teach us there's nothing absolute in this world. They want everyone to compromise—to be a 'team player.' But the Bible says you can't serve two gods: it's either God or mammon. And in the banking industry, I think we know which god is involved."

He picked up a newspaper clipping from his October press conference. "Here it is," he said, reading the headline aloud: " 'Christian Farmer Goes to Court to Fight the Devil's Agents.' That's pretty accurate, don't you think?"

A generation after the War of 1812, George's great-grandfather, a Scottish immigrant named John Bothwell, purchased one hundred acres just outside of Owen Sound. He set to taming the formless wilderness, clearing the land of trees and raising an elegant three-story French Renaissance farmhouse. Limestone from the escarpment was put to manifold uses: large blocks set the foundation for the barn; mixed with water, it became a disinfectant and whitewash; ground up in a rough paste, it bound walls together as plaster and mortar. Thin wedges of slate kept the rain off their heads.

For George's great-grandfather, the escarpment was a brute fact of life; as tough and remorseless as his Calvinism, it was the ground beneath his feet. Industrialists saw things differently. To them, the escarpment was a hindrance to progress, a barrier to trade. In 1824, engineers broke the ancient rocky spine to build the Welland Canal, a series of forty locks that permitted the free flow of goods between the upper and lower Great Lakes. Within two generations, modernization had begun to advance on the cultural confidence of evangelicals. Colleges and public life became less hospitable to open expressions of faith, while an influx of Catholic and Jewish immigration threatened the cultural monopoly evangelicals had long enjoyed. Under pressure, their pliant and fertile piety began to harden into an unyielding granite. Believers fought a rearguard action, retreating to higher ground and praying that divine intervention or popular uprising might turn back the enemy.

Sometimes, the fight against the Antichrist can get lonely. Even a freelance fundamentalist such as George likes company. When he talks about the photo-license issue, George often brings up the Amish. "Traditionalist" groups such as Old Order Amish and Mennonites reject photography as a violation of the second commandment: "Thou shalt not make graven images."

Before the terrorist attacks of 9/11, such groups were usually granted an exemption from photo requirements for documents such as passports and driver's licenses. In 2004, however, this policy of tolerance ended when a Canadian Amish man was turned back at the U.S. border for failing to have proper photo identification.

George's fundamentalism is very different from the Amish worldview. For starters, the Amish prohibition on graven images is absolute. George's issue with digital photography, and with technology in general, is selective, a matter of right and wrong usage. He has a computer and an e-mail address; his parlor walls are filled with family photographs. The bookshelves in his office are crowded with books like *Pastured Poultry Profits* and *Modern Corn Production*. In George's mind, there's nothing satanic in the coding of a JPEG, unlike the secret messages some think are recorded backward on "Stairway to Heaven." It's just that he'd rather not have his biometrics served up to the Antichrist on a silver platter.

Distinguishing between fundamentalists and traditionalists is important for understanding the range of religious responses to modernity. Traditionalists such as the Amish live in separatist enclaves, tightly adhering to community rule and premodern ways of doing things. George opposes some distinctive features of modern life, such as the move to consolidate and centralize authority. But he is also a product of the world he resists so militantly. George's gospel is radically individualistic rather than communal, self-consciously militant rather than taken for granted. It differs markedly not only from that of the Amish but from the Calvinism of his great-grandfather. George does not represent a return to the

Dark Ages, a time when faith in God was assumed. What he represents is an alternate way of being modern.

While George doesn't like to call himself a prophet, he is fond of the image of a watchman on the city walls. "You know, I believe I see somebody coming on the horizon there, and so I'm shouting to everybody inside. And the people are all down there partying and telling the watchman to shut up. So, when the authorities finally come along and shoot that guy and kick him off the wall, everybody kind of lets off a sigh of relief, because they don't have to listen to his crap anymore."

George can sometimes feel lonely in his crusade—a leader without followers, a lone voice in the wilderness separated in equal measure from the Amish, "Rapture-ready" Baptists, and his secular neighbors. Not even his own family sees eye-to-eye on the photo-license issue. When I first called George's house, his teenage daughter, Mary, answered the phone. "You want to speak to my father about his *theories*?" she asked quizzically.

"It's a strange thing," George said. "I seem to have personal relationships with people. I'm sure they talk among themselves, maybe they say some derogatory things, but I think they have this gnawing in their conscience, like there's a little more truth to what this guy's saying than we really wish there was. It's like that headline from the local paper: 'Bothwell Fights the Good Fight.' Now, it's *Bothwell* fighting, okay?—*we're* not part of it." He laughs. "But apparently it's a good fight."

Chapter 6

CHOSEN PEOPLE

S HALOM!"

The gate attendant greeted visitors as they passed beneath the faux-stone archway, modeled on Jerusalem's Jaffa Gate, which serves as the main entrance to the Holy Land Experience. Since 2002, the $12 million, fourteen-acre theme park in Orlando, Florida, has offered fundamentalists an Epcot of their own, a godly alternative to the secular entertainments of nearby Disney World and Universal Orlando Resort. Believers are shown re-creations of Christ's tomb, the Qumran Caves in Jordan (where the Dead Sea Scrolls were discovered), and a two-thirds-scale model of Herod's Temple, the epicenter of Judaism until its destruction by the Romans in A.D. 70. Throughout the day, these and other sites around the park become stages for Broadway-style mini-musicals performed by a young, sandal-shod troupe. The lineup of shows changes from season to season, but an average day climaxes at 4:25 p.m. with the passion play *Behold the Lamb*, during which three Roman soldiers kick and prod a blood-spattered Jesus, played by former airplane mechanic Les Cheveldayoff, to the top of an artificial hill, where he is stripped, fixed to a cross, and raised into place by a hydraulic motor.

Jonathan Hickey and George Livings, the park's resident Gilbert and Sullivan, pride themselves on the research that goes into their musical dramas. A team of biblical scholars—the "Bible boys," as they're affectionately known—screen each script for historical inaccuracies. For *The Wedding at Cana*, which tells the story of Jesus' first miracle, the producers scoured the Talmud to ensure the actors said the correct vows during the marriage scene. They also did research into the chuppah, the ceremonial canopy under which the bride and groom are wed. Jewish music from the period proved harder to pin down, so they set the piece to klezmer, a style born in the shtetlach of late-medieval eastern Europe. The decision proved a hit with the audience. During the show, a smiling, middle-aged woman visiting from Detroit leaned over and whispered, "I just love Jewish music."

In 2007, the Holy Land Experience was purchased by Trinity Broadcasting Network, the fundamentalist media empire of Pat Robertson, but it still bears the thumbprint of its founder, Marvin Rosenthal. Rosenthal is a Messianic Jew, which means that he recognizes Jesus as the Messiah but continues to observe the religious traditions of Judaism, including submission to the Torah. (As of 2003, there were roughly 400 Messianic synagogues around the world, 150 of them in the United States. An estimate from 1993 put the U.S. population of Messianic Jews at around 160,000.[1]) Rosenthal's cultural hybridity dictated the park's original twofold mission: to bring Jews to Christianity and to bring Christians to an appreciation of the Jewish roots of their faith.

In every corner of the Holy Land Experience, care was taken to present Christianity and Judaism as bosom friends. In the

Jerusalem Marketplace, the park's outdoor shopping plaza, Christian kitsch shared shelf space with Jewish tchotchkes. Elderly visitors in sun visors and Bermuda shorts perused kosher cookbooks and olive-oil soap from Israel, along with serious ritual items such as kippas, mezuzahs, prayer shawls, and velvet-robed Torah scrolls. A key chain based on the symbol for Messianic Judaism—a Star of David that morphs into a menorah on one side and a Christian fish on the other—captured the syncretistic mood.

One Jewish tradition paid particular attention is the Passover seder, the annual feast that commemorates the exodus from Egypt. Each year, the park hosts a series of Passover Seder Dinner Banquets, in which guests are treated to "Hebraic dancing" and a "Seder-tasting," with grape juice served in place of wine. The banquets have now become so popular that they run for four nights. In the lead-up to Passover, the park hosts a daily half-hour lecture on the seder meal in the Shofar Auditorium. During one presentation led by George Fredericks, one of the Bible boys, he asked how many in his audience had attended a seder. More than a third raised their hand. Fredericks encouraged them to consider hosting one themselves. "You can actually do it very easily in your home," he said.

As recently as a generation ago, fundamentalists would have been as likely to host a seder as to attend a Catholic mass. What explains the sudden passion for Judaica? One explanation could be the contemporary quest for "ethnicity." In recent years, many Americans disturbed by a lack of cultural depth in their lives have undertaken a quest to reconnect with "lost" ethnic roots: witness the popularity of shows such as *Riverdance* among people claiming one-quarter Irish ancestry. Some fundamentalists may be turning to Jewish culture in a similar way. In shows like *Wedding at Cana*, klezmer and Hebraic dancing provide believers an escape from contemporary Protestant worship with its knockoffs of mainstream popular culture. In philo-Semitism—a love of all things Jewish—believers can cultivate a taste of the exotic while skirting the relativism of liberal multiculturalism.

Not all fundamentalists are content to limit their exposure to "Jewish roots" to a theme park. Rudy Stockton is a firefighter from Bradenton, Florida. He keeps his longish black hair feathered back on the sides, and his body is solid and compact, creating the impression of strength held in reserve. Rudy got saved through a local Baptist church when he was in his twenties, which precipitated an interest in biblical prophecy. One day, while he was studying the book of Revelation, he came to a verse that confused him: "And he hath on his garment and on his thigh a name written, King of Kings, and Lord of Lords."

Rudy had been taught to take the plain, surface meaning of Scripture whenever possible, but in this case the literal sense made no sense. Why would Jesus have God's name written on his leg? Rudy took his question to the Internet. He figured out that the verse referred to the tzitzit, the Jewish prayer shawl, which, when draped around the neck, falls to midthigh. He also learned how one end of the shawl terminates in a series of long fringes knotted into coils, and how, according to Jewish tradition, when the coils are counted in a particular way, the numbers spell out the four-letter name of God.

"That's when it dawned on me," Rudy said. "These are Jews doing Judaism." Rudy tracked down everything he could find about the Jewish roots of Christianity. His investigation led him to the doorstep of Rabbi Gary Beresford, the leader of Ohr Yeshua, a Messianic congregation in Bradenton that rents space in the back of a local Protestant church. Rudy told Beresford about his fear that Christians had lost their ability to understand the Bible. "The true Messiah has been lost," he said. "The devil's goal is to take the Torah away. It always has been. If you take away the Torah—if you don't know what Jesus is supposed to look like—dressed in the tzitzit, and everything else—you're not going to know who he is, so you could end up following the Antichrist."

Rudy wanted to come to Beresford's synagogue, but first he needed to be assured that he would not feel out of place. Beresford assured him he would not. Aside from the rabbi and his wife, Ohr Yeshua's two dozen members were all gentiles like Rudy. Rudy showed up on the next Shabbat. Someone handed him a yarmulke and a tzitzit. Beresford opened with a prayer in Hebrew, and the congregation sang several hymns in Hebrew and English accompanied by a portable CD player. Rudy felt right at home.

Messianic gentiles such as Rudy have found a novel solution to the ancient Christian problem of the Jews: rather than wait for the Jewish people to embrace Christianity, he has embraced Judaism. Rudy submits himself to the Torah, observing holidays such as Yom Kippur and Hanukkah. He buys foods marked with a K or U and studies Torah whenever he can. Yet, unlike Orthodox Jews, he doesn't bother to separate milk and meat since, he says, the literal letter of the law prohibits only the boiling of a calf in its mother's milk. "Am I perfect?" he says. "No. But I try and do as much as I can. The Torah is like an onion: you do it layer by layer. You do it as you learn it. It's not meant to be a burden."

Perhaps the earliest problem in Christianity is the continued existence of Judaism. Shortly after Jesus' death, when it became clear that most Jews would not recognize Jesus as the Messiah, the early Christians went into damage control. Matthew's gospel shifted the blame for the crucifixion from Pilate, who ordered the execution, onto a Jewish crowd that cried out, "His blood be on us and on our people!" After the Roman Empire adopted Christianity, life became more difficult for the Jews than it had been under the pagan emperors. They suffered pogroms, forced conversions, and mass expulsions. Catholic theologians developed a doctrine known as supersessionism, which asserted that the Church had replaced the Jews as God's chosen people. In Jerusalem, Christians turned the holiest site in Judaism, the Temple Mount, into a garbage dump.

The Reformation showed initial promise for an improvement in Jewish-Christian relations. Early in his career, Martin Luther expressed a great deal of affection for the Jews, who, like him, had endured persecution at the hands of the Catholic Church. In 1523, Luther wrote the medieval equivalent of John F. Kennedy's "Ich bin ein Berliner" speech: "That Jesus Christ Was Born a Jew." It was a bold pledge of solidarity with Jewry against their common enemy. "The Jews are blood-relations of our Lord," Luther wrote. "If it were proper to boast of flesh and blood, the Jews belong more to Christ than we. I beg, therefore, my dear Papist, if you become tired of abusing me as a heretic, that you begin to revile me as a Jew."

Luther was convinced that once the Catholics had been defeated and Christianity purified, the Jews would finally flock to embrace the gospel. He was bitterly disappointed. Later in life, Luther turned violently against his former allies. In 1543, he wrote *On the Jews and Their Lies*, a masterpiece of anti-Semitic spleen. The Jews were "base, whoring people, that is, no people of God, and their boast of lineage, circumcision, and law must be accounted as filth." Luther sanctioned the burning of synagogues, mass expulsions, and worse. "We are at fault," he wrote, "in not slaying them."

Jewish sentiment in the New World bore deep contradictions. The few Jews who lived among the Puritans were prohibited from voting, holding office, or building synagogues, while their ancient ancestors, the Israelites, were afforded a respect that bordered on hero worship. In the Old Testament story of the Exodus, the Puritans saw a reflection of their own watery passage across the Atlantic. Leaders pilfered the storehouses of the Old Testament to name their towns and children. They sang hymns from the Psalms, taught Hebrew in their schools, and fashioned their legal statutes upon the stone tablets of the Mosaic Law. They even followed Jewish rules in observing the Sabbath, beginning at sundown the previous day. While suspicious of Jews, the Puritans were besotted with the Hebrews.

These contradictions bled down into the mid-nineteenth century, when Christian interest in the Jews began to migrate from the past to the future. In England and America, Protestants rallied for the restoration of the Jewish people to Palestine after two millennia of exile. This support, known as Christian Zionism, grew out of the fundamentalist system of biblical interpretation known as dispensationalism. Dispensationalism made the Jews into a hinge of cosmic history. First, the Jews would reoccupy the Holy Land and rebuild the temple in Jerusalem, activities that would precipitate the Rapture of the church. An Antichrist would rule for seven years, destroying the rebuilt temple and liquidating two thirds of the Jews in a holocaust. Jesus himself would save the remnant by returning in power and defeating the Antichrist. In gratitude, the Jews would hail Jesus as the Messiah. Jerusalem would become the seat of a new empire promising a thousand years of peace and plenty.

No early fundamentalist was more important to the spread of Christian Zionism than W. E. B. Blackstone. A dispensationalist and self-taught prophecy scholar from Illinois, Blackstone once traveled to the ancient ruins of Petra, in present-day Jordan, to bury thousands of Bibles in the sand, based on his belief that the Jewish remnant would gather there after fleeing the Antichrist. In 1878, Blackstone wrote a short tract called *Jesus Is Coming* that became the bestseller of the decade, selling more than a million copies. The booklet argued for Jewish statehood two decades before the first Zionist Conference in Basel, Switzerland. In 1890, he organized the first conference between Christians and Jews, in Chicago. When the Zionist leader Theodor Herzl wavered in his support for Palestine as the best home for a future Jewish state, Blackstone mailed him a copy of the Old Testament marked up with every reference to the Holy Land.

While other Christian Zionists were willing to wait for God's good time, Blackstone wanted to give history a nudge. Following the Russian pogroms of the 1880s, Blackstone sponsored a memorial sent to the desk of President Benjamin Harrison. Beginning with the question "What shall be done for the Russian Jews?" Blackstone offered a simple solution:

> Why not give Palestine back to them again? According to God's distribution of nations, it is their home—an inalienable possession from which they were expelled by force . . . We believe this to be an appropriate time for all nations, and especially the Christian nations of Europe, to show kindness to Israel. A million exiles, by their terrible sufferings, are piteously appealing to our sympathy, justice and humanity. Let us now restore to them the land of which they were so cruelly despoiled by our Roman ancestors.[2]

The resolution garnered the signatures of some of the most prominent Americans of the day, including a U.S. senator, the chief justice of the Supreme Court, John D. Rockefeller, the Speaker of the House of Representatives, and the mayors of New York, Chicago, and Boston. Though the memorial failed, Blackstone took hope from rising levels of Zionist emigration to Palestine, a land that he perceived (incorrectly) as unpopulated: after "eighteen centuries of dispersion, behold an astonishing anomaly on earth— a Land without a people and a people without a Land."

Blackstone believed not only that God intended to restore the Jews to Israel, but that he would use American Christians to do it. At the turn of the twentieth century, the United States welcomed unprecedented levels of Jewish immigrants from eastern Europe. Blackstone connected the words of Isaiah 11, which speaks of the gentiles helping to return a Jewish remnant to Israel, to those of

Isaiah 18, which suggests that this return will be carried out by sea. In the way that England was the staging ground for the invasion of France on D-day, American ships would establish a Jewish beachhead in the Promised Land.

Throughout the twentieth century, Christian Zionists would laud the prescience of Blackstone's predictions. During World War I, the British Crown signaled its favor of the establishment of a Jewish homeland in Palestine by means of the Balfour Declaration. In 1917, the Allies prized Palestine away from the Ottomans. For the first time since the Crusades, the Holy Land was under Christian control. To celebrate the victory, a British army under General Sir Edmund Allenby paraded through the streets of Old Jerusalem. Two decades earlier, a section of the city's ancient land wall had been razed before a visit by the German kaiser, who insisted that he enter Jerusalem on horseback. In contrast, Allenby was reluctant to invoke the messianic associations of a mounted conqueror riding into the City of David and walked humbly on foot beside his troops.

When the UN formally recognized the state of Israel in 1949, bringing to an end two millennia of peripatetic Jewish existence, Christian Zionists greeted the news as the direct fulfillment of prophecy. The same reaction followed the Six-Day War of 1967, when the Israeli Defense Forces obliterated the combined military mass of Egypt, Jordan, and Syria. Fundamentalists credited Israel's victories to the same hand that crushed Pharaoh's army in the Red Sea. The Israeli capture of East Jerusalem and the Temple Mount fueled a hurricane of millennialist speculation. Fundamentalist books and publications issued a stream of predictions concerning when Israelis might rebuild the temple and begin offering daily sacrifice.

Christian Zionism remains strong in America. In a poll from 1991, more than a third of those who support Israel said they do so because the Bible teaches that the Jews must possess their own country in the Holy Land before Jesus can return. In another survey, 63 percent of white evangelicals said that the modern state of Israel fulfills biblical prophecy about the Second Coming (while 58 percent of mainline Protestants said that it does not). Fundamentalist churches and organizations have raised millions of dollars to help Jews from Russia and African countries move to Israel to perform aliyah. One such group, the International Fellowship of Christians and Jews, was listed in 2003 as the second-largest charitable foundation in Israel. Televangelists such as Benny Hinn, Pat Robertson, and John Hagee encourage their flock to vote for candidates for Congress and the White House who will maintain a pro-Israel foreign policy.

In the past, fundamentalists defended their support for the Jews by pointing to the shared threat that communism presented to America and Israel. These days, the common enemy is militant Islam, a religion whose values believers contrast with those of "Judeo-Christian culture." Jewish response to these overtures of friendship has been divided. Israelis have in general been willing to overlook troubling aspects of fundamentalist theology in exchange for financial and political support. However, some Jewish groups are questioning the wisdom of collaborating with an ally who views the future prospects of the Jewish people as a choice between Christianity and a second Holocaust. Fundamentalists have assuaged these fears by downplaying the importance of End Times beliefs to their support of Israel. As proof of their good intentions, they quote the Old Testament passage where God tells Abraham that he "will bless those who bless you and curse those who curse you." But as the case of Luther illustrates, what starts out sounding like a blessing can later end up as a curse.

A half hour before the morning showing of *Wedding at Cana*, the performers of the Holy Land Experience assembled in a green-room just off the Jerusalem Marketplace. The atmosphere was festive, like that of a college dorm. Men and women, ranging in age from early twenties to mid-thirties, chatted, joked, and sang warm-up exercises. The newest member, Scott, had been with the troupe only a few months. Like the other male performers, he was handsome, trim, and affable. Unlike them, he was clean-shaven. "I'm a little less Jewish than the rest of my colleagues because I don't grow the facial hairs," he said. "It's embarrassing. I started to grow the beard and then they said, 'Uh, shave.'"

For the previous eight years, Scott worked just down the road at Disney World. He took a pay cut for his new job, and his faith had profited. "When you're out in the secular world, you're on your own," he said. "Usually you go to church to get rejuvenation, to be with like minds, to fellowship. I fellowship all week."

For many believers, a visit to the Orlando site is a surrogate pilgrimage, a chance to put flesh on the stories of the Bible. Though the exhibits are fake, the emotions they generate are real. "The first time my mother came here," said Scott, "she started crying when she walked into Temple Plaza, because she saw it standing as it was in Jesus' day. A lot of people come here to experience those feelings."

Some aspects of Scott's new job took getting used to. Initially, he felt uncomfortable greeting guests with "Shalom." "I was like,

'Well, I'm a Christian. Should I be saying *shalom*? I don't know about that.'" When a staff member explained that the word means "peace" in Hebrew, Scott decided he was okay with it. "I didn't realize how much stuff in the Jewish faith is in Christianity."

One of the most popular "Jewish roots" attractions at the Holy Land Experience is the Wilderness Tabernacle, a multimedia presentation on the "tent of meeting" that God commanded the Israelites to build during their forty years of wandering in the desert. Scott became excited telling the story of a woman who had spent years studying the tabernacle before making a special trip to Orlando for the twenty-minute show, in which an actor, dressed in the white robes and headgear of a Levitical priest, mimes the rites of animal sacrifice in front of a partial reproduction of the tent. The show climaxes inside the Holy of Holies, the sacred room that held the Ark of the Covenant. Lasers and sound effects produce thunder and lightning, while high-powered jets spray sheets of fog to evoke the pillar of cloud that led the Israelites through the desert and concealed the Shechinah, the Hebrew word for the divine presence.

"Oh, I love it when they do the Shechinah glory," said Scott. "That's awesome."

When I was growing up Brethren in the 1970s and 1980s, the Israelites and their ancient rituals were objects of devoted study. Particular attention was paid to the Tabernacle. Every element was mined for Christian typology. The golden menorah, the altar of incense, the brazen altar, the laver, right down to the threads that made up the twinings of the ropes that held the posts that secured the tent's outer perimeter—each element was a piece in a jigsaw puzzle that, when properly assembled, gave you a preview of the Messiah.

Some brothers carried their devotion further than others. We called them Tabernacle men. In another life, they might have spent weekends exchanging musket fire in re-created battles at Gettysburg and Appomattox. Using the book of Exodus as a manual, they built models of the Tabernacle out of balsa wood, twine, and old curtains. Itinerant preachers carried them from town to town. There's one I remember, a strange dollhouse four feet long and full of tiny painted furniture. I closed my eyes and pretended to be the high priest on the Day of Atonement, my hands trembling as I passed into the Holy of Holies and beheld the Ark of the Covenant and the twin golden cherubim that flanked the Mercy Seat. I'd pretend to utter God's secret four-letter name, YHWH, and cast the blood on the curtain in the prescribed manner as a propitiation for our sins.

One Tabernacle man's commitment was unsurpassed. He spent long evenings stitching the robes and voluminous turban of the high priest. He used four colors of thread to weave a Breastplate of Judgment and then fit it with fake gemstones, twelve in all, one for every tribe of Israel. He baked loaves of un-leavened bread and stacked them on his reconstruction of the Table of Shewbread. When he slipped on his robes and hung the heavy breastplate around his neck, he could imagine the inhos-pitable wastes of the Sinai Peninsula circa 500 BC: his face and hair coated in sand, his ears heavy with Hebrew, his nostrils re-plete with the sweet smoke of the burnt offering.

Our love of the Tabernacle was but one form of our deep identification with the Israelites. Like them, we were strangers in a strange land, a faithful remnant wandering the wilderness of modern life. We knew what it felt like to be called from the pack, to carry a blessing that weighed like a curse. For us, the Old Testament held more than ancient lore. It was our birthright as chosen people.

The first Holy Land attraction in America was Palestine Park, built in 1874 in Chautauqua, New York, by John Vincent. The park consisted of a 350-foot topographic model of Israel, complete with its own Jordan River; a small lake doubled as the Mediterranean shoreline. Visitors were encouraged to don Middle Eastern garb as they toured the park, which included a model of the Tabernacle. After returning from a pilgrimage to the Holy Land, Vincent became convinced that the development of a mature Christian faith required an understanding of Middle Eastern geography. So great was Vincent's desire to import the Holy Land to America that he arranged for shipments of rock, earth, and timber from Syria.

In 1904, the St. Louis World's Fair carried Vincent's dream to the next level. As the capstone of the fair, which marked the centenary of the Louisiana Purchase, organizers planned a special Jerusalem Exhibit: "The display will, in short, be Jerusalem itself," they wrote. The exhibit almost matched the size of Old Jerusalem: eleven acres carefully contoured to mirror the city's topography. Twenty-two streets were built, with three hundred houses, not to mention re-creations of the Jaffa Gate, the Church of the Holy Sepulchre, the Dome of the Rock, the Golden Gate, the Via Dolorosa, the Mount of Olives, the Garden of Gethsemane, the Wailing Wall, and the Tomb of David. Visitors rode on camels, shopped for wares in the souk, and eyed with curiosity the thousand real-life Palestinian peasants brought over to populate the Potemkin village.

In some ways, Orlando's Holy Land Experience is not so different from these earlier efforts. At the simplest level, they "bring the Bible to life." Dan Hayden, executive director of the Holy Land Experience, said that his goal was to give visitors "a sensory experience of biblical truth." For those believers for whom the Middle East is too remote, expensive, or dangerous to visit, Orlando offers a safe proxy for pilgrimage.

But Holy Land theme parks are about more than walking in the footsteps of Jesus. They are places where believers can witness the authority of Scripture in matters of geography, archaeology, and history. While modernity has made it easier for American believers to visit Israel, it has also brought serious challenges against the accuracy of the Bible, including its description of the Holy Land. When pilgrimage became popular in the later nineteenth century, owing to advances in transatlantic travel, many Americans went expecting to have their faith in the Bible tested. Philip Schaff, who visited in 1877, was relieved to find his fears misplaced:

> I found the country and the people pretty much as I expected, but I trust I understand both better than before. My faith in the Bible has not been shaken, but confirmed . . . There is a marvelous correspondence between the Land and the book. The Bible is the best handbook for the Holy Land, and the Holy Land is the best commentary on the Bible.[3]

For contemporary fundamentalists, the Holy Land Experience provides a similar confirmation of biblical truth—and if the Bible is right about the past, then it can be trusted in what it says about the future. Archaeology, for fundamentalists, is more than stones and bones: it is an expression of millennial hope, a preview of things to come. When Rosenthal built his Holy Land, he placed at its heart a six-story re-creation of Herod's Temple. For Christian Zionists, the temple offers a safe way to celebrate their Jewish roots. It looks back to a golden age before the noble race of Israelites fell from grace and became the Jews, a people cursed to wander the earth for rejecting their Messiah. But Rosenthal's monument also points to prophecies of a rebuilt temple at the end of history, when a remnant Jewish nation will bend the knee to Jesus, bringing final closure to an ancient Christian problem.

Back in the Shofar Auditorium, George Fredericks continued his presentation on the symbolism of the Passover seder. "Remember that the first churches were all Jewish people, and basically they were participating in this," he said. "What better holiday to interject symbols of the Messiah who had come?" He explained that the red wine traditionally served could symbolize Christ's blood, the means of atoning for sin, while the roasted egg, one of the six items arranged on the seder plate, stood for the "new birth" in Jesus. When he picked up the matzo bread, Fredericks remarked that the characteristic dark lines baked into its sides "remind us of the stripes that were placed on Christ's back" by Roman whips.

Fredericks then explained the tradition of the *afikomen*, in which the host breaks a piece of matzo into thirds, one of which is wrapped in a cloth and hidden until after dinner, when the children are sent off to hunt for it. "*Afikomen* means 'He came,'" said Fredericks. "Here's my suggestion: the top piece is the Father, the middle piece is the Son, and the bottom piece is the Holy Spirit. Jesus came, he was broken, he was hidden in the tomb. When he was found after his resurrection, there was great joy."

Fredericks closed his presentation by asking everyone to stand. He explained the custom of ending each seder with the last line of the Haggadah, "Next year in Jerusalem." The text of the Haggadah was compiled during the Middle Ages, when Jews in the Diaspora dreamed of returning in peace to the land promised to Abraham. "Now I know this isn't Jerusalem," said Fredericks, "but this is the Holy Land—we're close. So I'd like you all to stand and say it along with me on the count of three. One, two, three!"

"Next year in Jerusalem!"

Chapter 7

IN THE BEGINNING

O N M A Y 2 6 , 2 0 0 7 , Ken Ham, the CEO of the largest creationist organization in the world, Answers in Genesis (AiG), cut the ribbon to open the Creation Museum, a $27 million creationist facility in Petersburg, Kentucky. Ham, who is in his late fifties, speaks in a thick Australian accent and favors a gray Abraham Lincoln beard. Before a thousand attendees, including 130 reporters, he thanked the devoted volunteers whose time and energy had made the museum a reality, including, he said, "the local secular humanist group, Free Inquiry."

Free Inquiry had been protesting AiG since the mid-1990s, when the creationist group announced plans for a museum in the Cincinnati area. At the time, AiG hoped to build a thirty-thousand-square-foot building in a remote farming area twenty minutes from the closest freeway. But Free Inquiry aroused enough local opposition to block the proposed rezoning of the property. Undeterred, Ham found an even better location: a fifty-acre plot directly facing a freeway and only minutes from the Cincinnati airport, which is within a one-hour flight of two thirds of the U.S. population. He also decided to double the size of his museum, to sixty thousand square feet.

Free Inquiry's campaign against the Creation Museum backfired in other ways. Before the public debacle, the project had been receiving a modest level of private donations. But news reports of AiG's troubles generated an outpouring of sympathy from fundamentalist groups across the country, including an anonymous $1 million gift. On opening day, the museum was already debt-free.

Before the Creation Museum, fundamentalists already had a number of smaller such institutions across the country. But Ham wanted a "destination" for creationists, a museum that could compete on equal terms with the great shrines of modern evolutionary science, such as New York's Museum of Natural History. The massive, rounded columns that line the building's exterior evoke a sense of that ambition and scale. Inside the lobby, exhibits parrot mainstream curatorial tastes: floor-length glass cases, tastefully lit, held biological and geological treasures such as gemstones, fossilized dinosaur eggs, and a meteorite.

A nearby video exhibit addressed the question of how similar types of animals came to occupy opposite ends of the earth, a pattern known in biology as disjunct ranges: "The distribution of wildlife poses some puzzles for modern biologists. Why do we find giant island tortoises on islands in the Pacific Ocean and ten thousand miles away in the Indian Ocean, but nowhere in between?"

The answer, the video suggested, may be found at Mount St. Helens. During the volcano's eruption in 1980, hundreds of thousands of Douglas firs were uprooted. Twenty-five years later, many of the logs remained afloat on nearby lakes. "If Noah's Flood ripped up every forest in the world, mats of trees probably stayed afloat for centuries," the narrator said. "As winds blew these enormous log mats in circular paths in the oceans, they would have served as rafts for animals to cross oceans."

Mount St. Helens is a font of theoretical inspiration for creationists. Another video display employed the volcano to explain the origins of the Grand Canyon. "Have you ever wondered where canyons come from?" the narrator asked. "We know that mudflows from the crater of Mount St. Helens carved this canyon out of soft rocks in only hours, and this canyon out of solid rock in less than four years. So how were canyons really formed?"

Rather than deny the modern scientific consensus that the Grand Canyon formed slowly over millions of years, AiG left the question open, suggesting an impasse between creationists and mainstream geologists. "Each side has its own theory and collects physical evidence to support it," the exhibit implied. "Who is to say which one is right?"

If the Creation Museum mines the template of conventional American museums, at other times it feels closer to a theme park. Full-size animatronic dinosaurs—more than eighty of them— thunder and claw at visitors; in the Special Effects Theater, high-tech seats convulse and spray mist at the audience during a re-creation of Noah's Flood. Here the museum comes off as a fundamentalist version of *Jurassic Park*. Such comparisons are fitting, given that the museum's designer, Patrick Marsh, also built the *Jaws* and *King Kong* exhibits at Universal Orlando Resort.

The Creation Museum is the crowning achievement of Ham's rapid consolidation of the growing American market in

Young-Earth Creationism, the belief that the entire universe was formed less than ten thousand years ago during six twenty-four-hour periods. In 1998, after four years in business, AiG already controlled 28 percent of the U.S. market in creationist materials, making it the country's second-largest player. Number one was Ham's former employer, the Institute for Creation Research (ICR), in Santee, California, which commanded 45 percent. Within two years, AiG had pulled ahead, and by 2004, Ham's organization had $10.5 million in annual revenue and a market share of 59 percent—most of which came at the expense of ICR, whose piece of the pie had shrunk to 20 percent. Over the same period, a handful of smaller creationist organizations also lost revenue to AiG.

Among the reasons for AiG's rapid ascent is Ham himself. His friendly, "no worries" demeanor belies his endless reserves of energy and savvy as a communicator. Under his direction, AiG has launched a glossy monthly magazine, *Answers*, produced home-school curricula, and marketed hundreds of books and DVDs on topics ranging from dinosaurs and Noah's Ark to astronomy, geology, particle physics, plate tectonics, and radiocarbon dating. As well as running AiG, which has branches in Canada and the UK, Ham has written or co-written twenty-one books (including *The Lie: Evolution* and children's titles such as *D Is for Dinosaur*), hosts a radio program broadcast on 850 stations, and leads dozens of creationism seminars every year.

Another reason behind the success of AiG is the way in which it markets creationism by linking it to fundamentalist opposition to abortion, euthanasia, pornography, and gay marriage. Creationism is sold as a philosophy of life, a worldview. AiG argues that whatever position you take in the evolution debate will predetermine your stance on moral issues in society. While the fight to defend "moral values" in society is important, AiG says, Christians will succeed in the culture war only when they devote as much energy to curing the disease at the heart of the modern project—evolution—as to alleviating its symptoms.

But perhaps the best reason that Answers in Genesis has captured American fundamentalism is its unconventional philosophy. Ham's empire preaches a forked gospel. On the one hand, AiG goes to great lengths to argue that "mainstream science confirms the Bible's history." At the same time, it questions the trustworthiness of all rational inquiry, presenting scientific knowledge, even creation science, as mere window dressing. "Ultimately, creationism and evolution have nothing to do with the evidence," Ham said. "It comes down to your presuppositions."

Ham's postmodern attitude represents a radical break from the pioneers of the modern creationist movement, which embarked in the 1960s on a quest for respect. Before then, it wasn't uncommon to hear reports of fundamentalist ministers who taught that dinosaur fossils had been buried in the ground by God to test the faith of believers. By taking up the tools and methods of science, the new breed of creationists believed they could demonstrate the factual basis of the biblical record.

Three decades later, the new creationists found themselves at a crossroads. Their efforts had won them little regard from America's ruling elites. Mainstream scientists ignored them, while judges consistently ruled against allowing creation science into the classroom. Ham felt a change in strategy was required. Creation science had failed, he said, because it made too many compromises with the world. Ham was particularly troubled by the Intelligent Design movement, which avoided all God-talk in order to bandy such philosophical ideas as "irreducible complexity." In trying to gain the world, creationism had lost its soul, the Bible.

The layout of the Creation Museum shows how Ham hopes to have it both ways. To enter the main exhibits, visitors pass through a "starting points" room, which re-creates the scene of a dinosaur dig. Two wax archaeologists kneel in the dirt as they work on exposing a fossil. A nearby video explains how the scientists are similar: each considers the same evidence and applies the same methods of observational science to what he sees. Yet, the narrator continues, the scientists have one important difference: their starting points. The first scientist begins by applying human reason. As a result, he concludes that the fossil is millions of years old and belongs to a species that evolved gradually from lower forms of life. The other scientist, who begins by acknowledging the authority of the Bible, concludes that the bones are six thousand years old and that they belonged to an animal whose ancestor was formed by God according to its *kind*—a biblical word that creationists prefer to *species*—on the sixth day of creation.

If all scientific conclusions are predetermined by prior commitments, then there is no fair way to judge between the competing claims of evolution and creationism. Science turns into religion, truth claims must be deconstructed or bracketed by a person's "worldview," and museums become theme parks—grand entertainments. After failing to beat modern science at its own game, fundamentalists such as Ham are employing a postmodern strategy in their 150-year contest with Charles Darwin. Like a player who crowds a chess board with checkers and marbles, creationists hope to sow enough confusion in the minds of the undecided to provoke a stalemate.

Science and religion have been in continental drift since the twelfth century, when the West rediscovered the writings of Aristotle. Like most ancient Greeks, Aristotle understood the universe to be eternal, a concept that contradicted Genesis and sent the trendy theological circles of Paris into a tizzy. Midway through the thirteenth century, the French philosopher Siger of Brabant came up with a novel solution. Siger was a medieval Jacques Derrida, a radical Aristotelian who took pleasure in deconstructing the philosophical certainties of his day. Counter to the assertion that all truth is one, a predilection that Christianity had inherited from Plato, Siger proposed the notion of a "twofold" or "double" truth: that a statement can be true in rational philosophy but false in religious belief. The orthodox were outraged. According to one account, Siger was stabbed to death with a pen—an end that his enemies considered fitting, since he had done so much damage with his own.

It took the greatest philosopher of the Middle Ages, Thomas Aquinas, to undo the discontent between reason and revelation. Aquinas's response to Aristotle was the *Summa Theologica*, a work that consumed decades of his life and miles of vellum (a recent edition comprises sixty volumes). Rather than offer a philosophical defense for the doctrine of creation, Aquinas argued that it was impossible for philosophy to prove or disprove either position. Christians knew that the world was not eternal, because God had revealed it to them in the Bible. Philosophical truth went back and forth like a tennis ball. Only faith could promise certainty.

In the centuries after Aquinas, Western scientists and philosophers pursued a path of increasing autonomy from the Church. During the Italian Renaissance, Galileo demonstrated the Copernican view that the earth revolves around the sun. Pope Urban VIII ordered Galileo to recant his position, which he did, and issued a ban on his scientific writings. It took a little more than a century for the Church to warm to heliocentrism, when Pope Benedict XIV lifted the ban on Galileo's work in 1741.

In Europe, the Galileo scandal epitomized the strained affections between science and religion. In the New World, however, the romance continued through force of habit into the nineteenth century. Real trouble did not arrive until the 1830s, when a Scottish geologist named Charles Lyell published *Principles of Geology*, a work that exploded the traditional Christian belief in a "young earth." Before Lyell, geologists generally agreed that the world was roughly six thousand years old—a number arrived at by adding up the genealogies of the Old Testament—and that its varied topography had been shaped through a chain of ancient catastrophes: floods, earthquakes, volcanoes, and the like. Lyell demonstrated that the earth's features resulted from the steady accumulation of small, uniform changes over enormous spans of time. His theory of uniformitarianism overthrew the reigning model, catastrophism, and raised a severe challenge to the reliability of Scripture.

With Lyell's demolition of the Bible's chronology, the new Protestant orthodoxy became Old-Earth Creationism, a compromise that tried in various ways to contort the Genesis story into the frame of modern geology. One method inserted a "gap" of millions of years between the first and second verses of Genesis 1, resulting in a two-stage creation process: an initial cosmic event that established the heavens and the earth, followed by a much later creation episode, when the various inhabitants of the Garden of Eden were formed over six literal days. Another popular approach, the "day-age" method, interpreted the six days of Genesis not as literal twenty-four-hour periods but as eras lasting thousands or millions of years. Neither solution was perfect. The gap theory accepted that plants and animals had died before the Fall of Adam, a notion directly contradicted by the Genesis narrative, while the day-age system had trouble explaining how the first plants survived without sunlight, which wouldn't be invented for at least another thousand years, on the fourth "day."

Lyell's greatest legacy was perhaps his influence on a young biologist named Charles Darwin, who encountered *Principles of Geology* en route to the Galápagos Islands on the HMS *Beagle*. Darwin carried Lyell's uniformitarianism even further, extending it into the origins of human life. When Darwin published *On the Origin of Species* in 1859, the immediate response of American religious leaders was muted in comparison to the Catholic reaction to heliocentrism two centuries earlier. The greatest American botanist of the day, Asa Gray, who was also a pious Christian, concluded that evolution did not conflict with faith. Protestant orthodoxy mutated once again, taking the form of "theistic evolution," which placed God's hand on the tiller of natural selection.

The modern tendency to speak of a "war" between science and religion is a relatively recent habit, born of the Scopes Monkey Trial of 1925. John Scopes's attorney was Clarence Darrow, then the most famous agnostic in the country. The prosecution was led by William Jennings Bryan, a devout Old-Earth creationist and three-time Democratic candidate for president.

The trial quickly became a media circus, with the entire nation focused on what reporters styled as a battle between two Americas: an urbanized North, representing reason, science, and social progress; and a rural South packed with yokels and superstitious "simians" whose benighted attachment to tradition threatened the upward march of American history. The climax of the trial took place on the final day of arguments, when the judge permitted Darrow to put Bryan, the defender of tradition, on the stand. For two hours, Darrow made Bryan look foolish, asking questions that highlighted the Bible's many contradictions and scientific inaccuracies. When Darrow asked Bryan where Cain got his wife, Bryan said that he did not know. When asked what would happen to the earth if the sun "stood still," as the book of Joshua recorded it had, Bryan again had no reply.

In the end, Scopes's conviction was a Pyrrhic victory for the antievolution movement, as media coverage of the trial turned public sentiment against the fundamentalists. In popular memory, Scopes became the creation myth of American modernity, when rationality and progress struck a deathblow against religious ignorance and demagoguery. Bryan gave the Scopes legend a fitting denouement when he died of natural causes a few days after the trial.

Yet the Scopes trial had not killed fundamentalism—only driven it underground. In 1961, two years after the centenary of Darwin's *Origin of Species*, a professor of engineering at Virginia Tech named Henry Morris launched the creationist revival with *The Genesis Flood*, a book that used scientific language and methods to defend a literal reading of Genesis. Morris brought catastrophism back into vogue, arguing that a global deluge from six thousand years ago could account for virtually all of the planet's sedimentary layers and fossil records. With *The Genesis Flood*,

Morris single-handedly saved Young-Earth Creationism, giving literalists a veneer of scientific respectability while avoiding the compromises of Old-Earth Creationism.

In 1970, Morris founded the Institute for Creation Research as the nerve center of the modern creationist movement. The institute developed its own graduate program, museum, and full-time staff of researchers with Ph.D.s who wrote papers with titles such as "Runaway Subduction as the Driving Mechanism for the Genesis Flood." That the center's research was never subjected to external peer review did nothing to hurt its popularity among believers. In the 1970s and 1980s, ICR researchers became minor celebrities for staging public debates with evolutionary scientists. The most famous was Duane Gish, a chemist who, in more than three hundred debates, would leap from claim to claim without responding to objections, a debating style that became known as the Gish gallop.

Gish, along with all creationists, was attempting to restage the Scopes trial, whose memory still haunted the movement half a century later. Creationists hoped that by turning the enemy's weapon against him, they might restore the Bible to a place of honor in American society. The Institute for Creation Research promised believers a new marriage of reason and revelation, a grand synthesis of truth.

Yet, even the father of the modern creationism began to doubt whether creation science could deliver on its big promises. After the institute failed in its repeated efforts to restore creation science to public schools, Henry Morris began to change his mind about whether science could offer a secure path to knowledge. Morris was influenced by the thought of Cornelius Van Til, a Dutch-born theologian who taught briefly at Princeton

Theological Seminary in the 1920s. Van Til challenged the view that human reason provided a common ground between believers and nonbelievers. Christianity, he said, is based not on reason but on the presupposition that the Bible is the Word of God.[1]

Some creationists feared that Morris's retreat from science threatened the movement's raison d'être. Morris's coauthor on *The Genesis Flood*, John Whitcomb, caviled at his putdown of creationism as "mere scientific theory." For Christianity to survive, Whitcomb argued, creationists had to restore the unity of truth. Science and faith, he argued, could not be isolated without inviting disaster.

Ken Ham, however, sided with Morris. Biblical presuppositions must go ahead of scientific evidence. In 1987, during a Supreme Court showdown over a Louisiana law that permitted schools to give "balanced treatment" to creation science and evolution, Ham got into hot water for saying in public that the scientific evidence for creationism didn't matter—it was all based on the Bible. One leading creationist told him to keep his mouth shut: "He said, 'You could undermine our whole case if they get hold of this.'" Ham was unchastened. "We lost anyway," he says, "which is what we predicted."[2]

Today, Ham has given up on the courts. Answers in Genesis does not support any legal effort to introduce creation science into public schools. Instead, it targets believers—churches, Christian schools, and home-school groups—a marketing strategy that allows AiG to be as biblically focused as it pleases. Ham believes AiG's domination of American creationism proves his point that creationists can succeed only if they play by their own rules, rather than conform to those set by the world. "When you take away your starting point of Scripture," Ham says, "you're left with their starting point—human reason. It's a situation where you can never win."

Over the last twenty years, belief in creationism has held more or less constant at the national level. In a 2004 Gallup poll, nearly half of Americans—45 percent—said that the Genesis account was literally true. A similarly high number, 38 percent, said that God somehow guided evolution. Only 13 percent held a purely naturalist view of evolution—meaning that God played no role whatsoever. For the vast majority of Americans, the heart of the creation-evolution debate is not a choice between atheism and fundamentalism, but between dueling creationisms.

One reason Americans may be reluctant to accept purely naturalist interpretations of evolution is that scientists themselves continue to express evolutionary concepts in the language of meaning and intention. Allen MacNeill, a professor of evolutionary biology at Cornell who taught a course examining the claims of Intelligent Design, admits that the paradox of purpose in nature is one that biologists have not yet solved. "What are evolutionary adaptations," he wrote, "if not structural and functional characteristics that serve a purpose in the life of an organism? While it sounds silly to say that rocks fall 'in order to' reach the ground, it doesn't sound silly to say that the heart pumps the blood 'in order to' circulate it throughout the body."[3]

Even a famous atheist such as Richard Dawkins can't resist the language of agency, meaning, and morality when discussing evolution. Consider the title of his bestselling book, *The Selfish Gene*, which puts an egocentric molecule in the driver's seat of natural selection. When the explanatory power of science fails, it leaves a vacuum that must be filled. Rational organisms require answers to life's basic questions. When physicists suggest that reality consists of elementary "strings" that can't be measured, or that 96 percent of the universe consists of something called dark matter whose existence can't be demonstrated, science offers us a picture of reality that confounds logic and demands an act of faith.

Young-Earth creationists such as Ham take advantage of these developments to argue that science is based on a set of presuppositions as religious as their own. Rather than acknowledge the broad range of presuppositions available between the extremes of literalism and materialism, their strategy is to take the middle path off the table. Either the Bible is a reliable guide to geology, biology, astrophysics, and genetics, or it is a pack of lies and fairy tales. The world can be an orderly cosmos fashioned by the hand of God in six days, or it can be a vacuum of chance and cruelty, where acts of genocide carry no moral weight. Believers, Ham says, must choose which world they want to live in.

Raising the stakes in the creation-evolution debate might convince many to stand on literalism, but in the case of younger, college-bound believers, such strategies may backfire. In a poll taken at evangelical Wheaton College in Illinois, 47 percent of students said they were Young-Earth creationists when they arrived, but only 27 percent continued to hold such beliefs at the time the survey was taken. According to AiG's estimates, more than 90 percent of professors at Christian colleges in America are not Young-Earth creationists. Only five regionally accredited colleges offer biology degrees oriented to Young-Earth beliefs, and none offer geology degrees with such an emphasis.

Faced with such trends, AiG devotes special energies to combating moderate models of creationism. Conferences and educational materials repeat the refrain that any compromise with evolution questions the integrity of a Christian's entire faith—including personal salvation. If evolution is correct, then there was no literal Adam; if there was no Adam, then there was no Fall; if there was no Fall, then there is no such thing as original sin. If that's true, then there is no need for atonement—for Jesus, the "second Adam," to have died on the cross. In a corner of the Creation Museum, a display tells the story of Charles Templeton, once a famous evangelist and close friend of Billy Graham. Later in life, Templeton wrote a memoir called *Farewell to God*, in which he described how he had abandoned faith after accepting the truth of evolution and other modern theories. The museum offers Templeton's fall as a cautionary tale, the Faustian bargain that awaits any believer foolish enough to make a deal with modernity.

In 1841, the father of modern geology, Charles Lyell, made his first visit to Niagara Falls. He traveled up and down the seven-mile gorge, taking measurements of the rock to calculate the rate of erosion and deduce an approximate age for the natural wonder. Locals shared stories of seeing massive chunks of limestone break off and fall into the gorge. "The sudden descent of huge fragments in 1818 and 1828 is said to have shaken the adjacent country like an earthquake," he wrote.[4]

When Charles Templeton abandoned the Bible, his fall produced similar shock waves among fundamentalists. But faith does not always fail so catastrophically. For the majority of his life, my mother's father was a Young-Earth creationist. In his seventies, he had a change of heart while reading a book about Niagara Falls. The author described how the falls had been produced by the collision of two ancient forces: the Niagara Escarpment, a long ridge of limestone left over from a tropical sea that once covered central North America; and the Niagara River, which transported the watery remains of a continental glacier from Lake Erie to Lake Ontario.

Without any dark night of the soul, my grandfather became an Old-Earth creationist. So far as he was concerned, the authority and accuracy of Scripture had not been compromised. It was a mistake, he said, to confuse God's Truth, which was forever and unchanging, with our limited ability to grasp it.

After that, I began to see him differently. His faith had always seemed as steady and constant as granite. But like all things under the sun, it changed with time. The river of human experience had rubbed many of his jagged edges smooth. His conviction that reason and revelation could harbor no lasting enmity, coupled with his inclination to take truth where he found it, encouraged him to synchronize the disparate rhythms of ancient myth and modern science. His faith resembled a handmade clock pieced together from odd, mismatched parts: bits of a sundial and a pendulum, coils of rope and wire springs, stone cogs meshing imperfectly with stainless-steel gears. Somehow, it kept time.

Epilogue

AFTER FUNDAMENTALISM

M Y GRANDFATHER DIED in 2007, the same year that Jerry Falwell, the most famous Christian fundamentalist in the world, passed from the stage. Had they ever met, I am sure the preachers would have found agreement on a number of issues, notably the inerrancy of Scripture, the dire state of American culture, and the imminence of the Rapture, which increased the pressure on believers to reach more souls with the gospel.

Yet, I am also certain they would have disagreed about nearly as much. My grandfather was a stalwart separatist who pled the incompatibility of Christianity with nationalism or political activity, which diluted a believer's focus on the kingdom of God. Falwell followed such a creed until the 1970s, when shifting public attitudes on abortion and homosexuality caused him to lead a cultural *reconquista* in American public life. He accused men like my grandfather of shirking their responsibility to the "cultural mandate" given in Genesis 1:28, a verse that, for some, asserts a Christian obligation to assume rule over every sphere of human activity.*

Despite such differences, no one could contest that either was a Christian fundamentalist, a fact that helps explain the movement's extraordinary growth. Fundamentalism is no monolith. Like the pointillist paintings of Georges-Pierre Seurat, its solid forms fragment and dissolve on closer inspection. Once believers move past a sacred ring of social values—opposition to gay marriage, abortion, pornography—they have difficulty reaching consensus. Many basic doctrines, such as belief in the Rapture or a Young Earth, remain deeply contested. These internal divisions, the fruit of a tradition that prizes the art of persuasion and places a responsibility on each believer to discern the will of God through prayer and private study of the Scriptures, are likely to multiply. Fundamentalism has no pope, no center of authority beyond the Bible. Having no center, it can by definition have no periphery. Anyone who professes a personal relationship with Jesus is entitled to interpret God's Word and to try to win an audience for his views. Fundamentalist faith is exciting and dynamic in part because it is a free-for-all—an unregulated sacred sprawl of freewheeling pastors and loosely bound churches and denominations.

Just as the fundamentalist world is no monolith, it is also more malleable than often acknowledged. A brittle outer crust protects its molten heart. Creationists defend a "biblical worldview" freed from the bonds of time and space, yet the power of organ-

---

*In the verse, God instructs Adam and Eve to "fill the earth and subdue it. Rule over the fish of the sea and the birds of the air and over every living creature that moves on the ground."

izations such as Answers in Genesis lies in the ability to assimilate outside influences, to change direction, to adapt to new intellectual environments. The creationism of Ken Ham blends mutually exclusive philosophies like a musician switching time signatures: postmodern attacks on truth and objectivity are turned inside out to support a literal reading of Genesis. To an unbelieving ear, fundamentalism is a rigid recital of dogma. But in the hands of a skilled improviser, it sounds more like jazz. The song remains the same, but the tune is restless, the tempo constantly changing.

This genius for harmonizing tradition and innovation is entering a new phase, one that may transcend earlier debates between separatists and activists over how to be in the world but not of it. Moving past the thesis and antithesis of separatism and activism, believers are embracing a pragmatic synthesis, a neofundamentalism that is simultaneously at home in American society and alienated from it.

If fundamentalists learned anything from the twentieth century, it is that the best way to resist the encroachment of modernity is by keeping pace with it. Masters of verisimilitude, they empty the wineskins of secular culture and fill them with grape juice. Believers produce polished knockoffs of Hollywood thrillers and MTV. They follow wrestlers with handles such as "the Sermonator" and "the Abrahammer." Their talking heads spin glosses on postmodernist theory. A network of private schools and colleges teaches the next generation a parallel curriculum of science and American history. Believers no longer have to choose between this world and the next. They have built a world within a world, a microcosm of American society that promises all the advantages of separatism without the staleness of quarantine, and all the benefits of modern life without the risk of contamination.

There was no single moment when I ceased to be a fundamentalist, no stroke of disenchantment, no deconversion. Like a train leaving a station, my departure was so incremental it is hard to say precisely when it happened.

At a basic level, I wanted more life. That's what Jesus promised his disciples, and it is what my grandparents found in the Brethren in the 1950s. Biblical faith provided an escape from the shallow streams of liberal optimism and secular materialism. The beauty of Scripture ennobled their lives and focused their devotion. Its wisdom corrected and consoled; its stories offered models and precursors with which to frame the events of daily life, making sense of tragedies and triumphs, twining their private destinies with that of the universe.

Because I respected their faith and the sacrifices they had made, I knew I could not settle for a poor photocopy of it. Like them, I had to make my own way to Damascus. For a teenager in the 1980s, the Brethren offered a closed window on the world. Jesus said that perfect love would cast out fear, but too often the saints seemed girded about with fears of impurity, change, and disappointment. By casting doubt as an act of treason or ingratitude rather than as a dialogue partner, the iron that sharpens the blade, they hoped to curb my natural curiosity about the world. But I did not share their lust for certainty. It was authenticity I wanted.

So I fell away. As a child of mixed parentage—a mother who submitted to the Protestant sacrament of conversion, a father who resisted—I'd always been in a halfway covenant with the

Brethren: in the saints but not of them. I left hoping to escape this split sense of identity, to find wholeness in the world. But I felt no more at home in the world than I had among the Brethren. The diasporic sensibility that my grandparents cultivated, the feeling of being a stranger in a strange land, still gripped me. I suffered from a spiritual arrhythmia that set a chamber of my heart beating out of time. Later, I saw how the modern condition was its own diaspora—a wilderness of self-alienation, futility, and dis-ease.

In my early adult life, I struggled to find a way to re-enchant the world, to reconcile the claims of tradition and modern life. I experimented with evangelical and mainline liberal churches but was frustrated by the informality of their worship and by the sunny revisionism that elided any doctrine of potential embarrassment to the modern mind (as John Updike said, "Too much light"). In its embrace of all things new, liberal Protestantism struck me as no less extreme than the fundamentalism I had fled. In the Brethren, I had bucked against the image of an angry and vengeful God. But the alternative, to cleanse God of all fierceness, was equally distasteful, a watery soup.

One day I wandered into an Anglican church, closing the circle on my grandfather's exodus more than sixty years before. I didn't feel that I had arrived so much as that I'd begun a process without an end. In ritual and liturgy I found a bottomless beauty that, though polar to the unscripted sermons of my childhood, mirrored in strange ways the patient and sober reverence of Brethren worship. I also began to discover the riches of theology. Reading the post-biblical traditions of the Church, I came to see how earlier believers had defined orthodoxy not in terms of purity but as a shifting point of balance between mutually undesirable extremes, a yoking of contraries, a third way.

In the first debates over Christ's nature, the defenders of purity staked out two mutually exclusive options: either Jesus was wholly divine, or he was a man like other men. The first option precluded his full humanity; the second ruled out his participation in the godhead. Occam's razor avers that reason always cuts to the simplest solution to a problem. But the earliest followers of Jesus, those who knew him most intimately, zigzagged. Their accounts sometimes describe a man who walked, talked, and suffered alongside his friends. But they also depict a presence that transcended our immanent frame and disclosed the taproot of life itself. Their experience told them what reason could not: that Jesus was both human and divine.

The eventual orthodox position, which asserted two equal natures, human and divine, rejected purity in favor of paradox. All too often in its history, the Church has allowed orthodoxy to be settled by swords and inquisitions rather than by the strivings of anxious seekers. Yet, in rare moments of genius, it has approximated what the ancient Greeks knew as the golden mean. As Aristotle put it, "It is best to rise from life as from a banquet, neither thirsty nor drunken." To pursue the mean is not to settle for tepid compromise but to chart a narrow course between Scylla and Charybdis, to skirt the twin dangers of excess and deficiency.

If fundamentalism has too often foundered on the shoals of purity, it has also known something of the open sea. Nearly two decades after leaving the Brethren, I find myself returning again and again through memory to its waters. I come back for its affirmation of daily life, for the love of literacy and lay study. I come back to be reminded that truth is not a popularity contest, that standing up for what you believe can set you against the powerful current of modern consensus. More often than not, this willingness to fight for the faith was tempered by the recognition of a believer's frightening limitations in the eyes of heaven. The Word of God might be fixed for all time, but its interpretation is never-ending, an unfinished third testament to which each believer contributes a verse. Truth comes not cold and perfect into the world. Ever an alloy of humanity and divinity, it must be fired and formed in the heart's forge, and the crude shapes that result offered up with humility.

NOTES

INTRODUCTION: THE F-WORD

1. George Marsden, *Understanding Fundamentalism and Evangelicalism* (Grand Rapids, MI.: W. B. Eerdmans, 1991), 98.

2. Martin E. Marty, "Morality, Ethics, and the New Christian Right," *The Hastings Center Report*, Vol. 11, No. 4 (August 1981), 14. See also H. Richard Niebuhr, *The Social Sources of Denominationalism* (Cleveland: The World Publishing Company, 1929).

3. Marsden, *Understanding Fundamentalism and Evangelicalism*, 57.

4. George Marsden, *Fundamentalism and American Culture: The Shaping of Twentieth-Century Evangelicalism, 1870–1925* (New York: Oxford University Press, 2006), 235.

5. See Ernest Sandeen, *The Roots of Fundamentalism: British and American Millenarianism, 1800–1930* (Chicago: University of Chicago Press, 1970).

6. G. K. Chesterton, *Orthodoxy* (Whitefish, MT: Kessinger Publishing, 2004), 86.

CHAPTER 1: WAITING FOR GOD

1. Sylvester Bliss, *Memoirs of William Miller* (Berrien Springs, MI: Andrews University Press, 2005), 256.

CHAPTER 2: THE WORD WAS GOD

1. Frank Newport, "One-Third of Americans Believe the Bible Is Literally True," Gallup News Service, May 25, 2007.

2. Dwight Pentecost, *Things to Come* (Grand Rapids, MI: Zondervan, 1965), 42.

3. Philip Mauro, *The Seventy Weeks and the Great Tribulation* (Boston: Hamilton Brothers, 1923), 9–12.

4. Charles C. Ryrie, *Basic Theology: A Popular Systematic Guide to Understanding Biblical Truth* (Chicago: Moody Publishers, 1999), 81.

5. Alexis de Tocqueville, *Democracy in America* (Garden City, NY: Anchor Books, 1969), 295.

6. John Nelson Darby, *Letters of John Nelson Darby*, Vol. 1, 1832–1868 (London: Stow Hill Bible and Tract Depot), 351.

7. William Kelly, "John Nelson Darby as I knew him," Sound Teaching on Electronic Media, http://www.stempublishing.com/authors/kelly/7subjects/jnd_knew.html.

8. T. T. Shields, *The Gospel Witness*, April 7, 1932.

CHAPTER 3: SAVED

1. Quoted in William James, *Varieties of Religious Experience* (New York: The Modern Library, 1936), 231.

2. James Hastings, "Conversion," *Encyclopedia of Religion and Ethics* (T. & T. Clark Publishers, 1926), 106.

3. Quoted in James, *Varieties of Religious Experience*, 224.

4. W. Somerset Maugham, *The Moon and Sixpence* (New York: Penguin Classics, 1993), 49.

5. Bruce Corley, "Interpreting Paul's Conversion—Then and Now," in *The Road from Damascus*, ed. Richard N. Longe-necker (Grand Rapids, MI: W. B. Eerdmans, 1997), 11.

6. Ibid.

7. Edmund S. Morgan, *Visible Saints: The History of a Puritan Ideal* (Ithaca, NY: Cornell University Press, 1965), 68–70.

8. Bruce Hindmarsh, *The Evangelical Conversion Narrative: Spiritual Autobiography in Early Modern England* (Oxford: Oxford University Press, 2005), 143.

9. James, *Varieties of Religious Experience*, 233.

10. Charles Grandison Finney, *Memoirs of Rev. Charles G. Finney* (New York: A. A. Barnes and Company, 1876), 12.

CHAPTER 4: THE PURSUIT OF PURITY

1. Augustine, *Confessions* (Oxford: Oxford University Press, 1991), 152–53.

2. Hannah Elliott, "Avoiding Other Vices May Make Baptists Fatter, Researcher Suggests," Associated Baptist Press, September 27, 2006, http://www.abpnews.com/1396.article (accessed July 31, 2007).

CHAPTER 6: CHOSEN PEOPLE

1. Roy H. Shoeman, *Salvation Is from the Jews: The Role of Judaism in Salvation History* (San Francisco: Ignatius Press, 2003), 351.

2. Quoted in Timothy Weber, *On the Road to Armageddon: How Evangelicals Became Israel's Best Friend* (Grand Rapids, MI: Baker Academic, 2004), 103.

3. Quoted in Gershon Greenberg, *The Holy Land in American Religious Thought, 1620–1948* (Lanham, MD: University Press of America, 1994), 106.

CHAPTER 7: IN THE BEGINNING

1. See Cornelius Van Til, *Christian Apologetics* (Phillipsburg, NJ: P&R Publishing, 2003).

2. Personal conversation with Ken Ham, May 14, 2007.

3. Allen MacNeill, "Riding the Evolution-Design Roller Coaster," The Evolution List, http://evolutionlist.blogspot.com/2006/04/riding-evolution-design-roller-coaster.html (accessed August 9, 2007).

4. Charles Lyell, *Principles of Geology*, 11th ed. (New York: D. Appleton and Co., 1873), 1:356.

ACKNOWLEDGMENTS

A number of people deserve special acknowledgment for assistance provided during the research and writing of this book. Amitav Ghosh, Barney Karpfinger, and Glen Smith provided early encouragement and editorial guidance, while my parents, Brenda and Malcolm Grainger, contributed crucial memories and the inestimable support of their blessing. The patient direction of Sarah Fulford and George Gibson, my editor at Walker & Company, helped teach a stuttering manuscript how to talk. Thanks go as well to the Canada Council for the Arts, Harvey Cox, Eric Gutierrez, David D. Hall, John Hannah, Jane Motz Hayes, Jonathan Hayes, Sarabinh Levy-Brightman, Stephen Marche, Krista Muir, Mark Noll, Meg and Barlow Patten, Stephanie Paulsell, Amelia Perkins, Patrick Provost-Smith, Sheila Smith, Charles Stang, John Thompson, and Jim Wallis. Lastly, it is enough to say that without Rachel, there would be no book.

A NOTE ON THE AUTHOR

BRETT GRAINGER has explored the intersection of religion and politics for a variety of magazines, newspapers, and public radio. He has been an editor at *Sojourners*, a magazine of religion, politics, and culture. Grainger holds a master's degree from Harvard Divinity School, where he studied global fundamentalist movements with Harvey Cox. He lives in Cambridge, Massachusetts, and this is his first book.